CHRISTIANITY:
TWO THOUSAND YEARS

CHRISTIANITY: TWO THOUSAND YEARS

edited by

Richard Harries

and

Henry Mayr-Harting

OXFORD
UNIVERSITY PRESS

OXFORD
UNIVERSITY PRESS

Great Clarendon Street, Oxford OX2 6DP

Oxford University Press is a department of the University of Oxford.
It furthers the University's objective of excellence in research, scholarship,
and education by publishing worldwide in

Oxford New York

Athens Auckland Bangkok Bogotá Buenos Aires Cape Town
Chennai Dar es Salaam Delhi Florence Hong Kong Istanbul Karachi
Kolkata Kuala Lumpur Madrid Melbourne Mexico City Mumbai Nairobi
Paris São Paulo Shanghai Singapore Taipei Tokyo Toronto Warsaw

with associated companies in Berlin Ibadan

Oxford is a registered trade mark of Oxford University Press
in the UK and in certain other countries

Published in the United States
by Oxford University Press Inc., New York

British Library Cataloguing in Publication Data

Data available

Library of Congress Cataloging in Publication Data
Christianity: two thousand years/edited by Richard Harries and Henry Mayr-Harting.
p. cm.
Includes bibliographical references
1. Church history. I. Harries, Richard. II. Mayr-Harting, Henry.
BR145.3.C47 2001 270–dc21 2001021920

ISBN 0-19-924485-5

1 3 5 7 9 10 8 6 4 2

Typeset by Joshua Associates Ltd., Oxford
Printed in Great Britain
on acid-free paper by
Biddles Ltd., Guildford & King's Lynn

INTRODUCTION

This book has its origins in a series of public lectures given in Oxford on the History of Christianity, over the academic year 1999–2000, to mark the end of the second millennium and the looking ahead to the third. The idea was to take stock of where Christianity was now and how it had got to that state. It seemed an appropriate way to celebrate the turn of the millennium. The suggestion for the lectures came from John Drury, Dean of Christ Church; it was taken up with enthusiasm by Richard Harries, Bishop of Oxford; and he then associated me with their organization. We did not ask lecturers to follow a particular brief other than that they might bring out in their period, in such a way as to appeal to non-experts, some elements of the creative contribution which that period had made to the development or fabric of Christianity. By 'creative contribution' we did not of course mean no criticisms; the Christian church has depended on criticism from outside and inside for much of its development. Our very broad brief was a tall order, and imposed a problem of selectivity, to be solved by each lecturer according to his or her own disposition and interests. The resulting book is one of very different approaches to the different periods. If that is partly because the various periods demanded it, it is also what one must expect when one asks experienced scholars, who have already developed their own intellectual personalities, to engage in a venture like this. No two pianists sound like each other unless they are amateurs.

(104689)

Nonetheless we are grateful to the publishers' readers for spotting at least two major themes which had largely slipped through the net, one the Jews and Jerusalem (this theme only after the first two contributions), the other the liturgy, Mass and baptism. To remedy this lack was clearly not something we could do by tinkering with the various chapters. On the Jews, Richard Harries, who is an expert on Jewish/Christian relations, is glad to have the opportunity to take up this matter in his closing contribution. Here I would only wish to point readers in the direction of literature which may help them to remedy this lack for themselves. On the importance of the pilgrimage to Jerusalem (connected of course with the Crusades), and the process of alienation between Christians and Jews in the Middle Ages, one could do well to start with Colin Morris, *The Papal Monarchy* (Oxford, 1989), pp. 277–81, 354–7; and the bibliography at p. 629. *The Oxford Illustrated History of the Crusades*, ed. Jonathan Riley-Smith (Oxford, 1995) is also to be recommended; and from the Jewish side, Joshua Prawer, *The Latin Kingdom of Jerusalem* (London, 1972).

Not two hundred yards from where I am writing this introduction, there is a stone plaque dated 1931 on the wall of the Town Hall on St Aldate's Street, Oxford, which reads:

This street known till 1300 as Great Jewry contained many houses of the Jews including the Synagogue which lay to the North of Tom Tower.

That is roughly where the Junior Common Room of Christ Church and the Lodgings of the Archdeacon of Oxford are today. The moving and sometimes harrowing story of Jewish relations with the townspeople and scholars of Oxford before the expulsion of the Jews from England in 1290 is vividly told in Cecil Roth, *The Jews of Medieval Oxford* (Oxford, 1951). It can be taken as a microcosm of the whole subject.

One can always tell where Jews have abounded in European history, from the evidence of anti-Semitism. Yet they were indispensable to Christians, and not only as moneylenders. They were indispensable to Christian scholars who took biblical scholarship seriously. And from the eighth century they became indispensable in another way. As Alexander Murray explains in this volume, the eighth century saw the break-up of the cultural and religious unity of the Mediterranean, a large part of its seaboard having come into the hands of the Muslims. Yet trading and cultural contacts built up apace between Christendom and Islam. The paternity of both these religions was Judaism, and so Jews acquired naturally the function of cultural as well as trading mediators between the two.

The subject of baptism is not ignored in our book, as the reader of Diarmaid MacCulloch's contribution will see, but in the period which I have written about it is, and that is a pity, because it was at that time, particularly in a missionary context, not only a ritual of initiation (and that was important enough) but also a major vehicle for expounding the Christian faith as a whole. This can be seen from Peter Cramer, *Baptism and Change in the Early Middle Ages c. 200–c. 1150* (Cambridge, 1993). As to the Mass, I doubt if Josef Jungmann's *Missarum Sollemnia* (2 vols), translated into English as *The Mass of the Roman Rite: its Origins and Development* by Francis A. Brunner (New York, 1951), is ever likely to be superseded. Theodor Klauser, *A Short History of the Western Liturgy* (Oxford, 1969) is also a brilliant book. Yet another masterpiece, dealing in its last chapter with the Anglican liturgy, is Gregory Dix, *The Shape of the Liturgy* (London, 1945). On a completely different approach, still with much mileage in it, is John Bossy, 'The Mass as a Social Institution, 1200–1700', in *Past and Present* no. 100 (1983), pp. 29–61.

It was an exhilarating experience to be an organizer of, and listen to, such a series of lectures. They were attended by audiences always in the hundreds, comprising scholars, students, and many interested members of the general public. Many were the appreciative comments which we received, not generally of individual lectures as if of a favourite singer in the performance of an opera, but of the series and its concept as a whole. That is a major reason why we have been encouraged now to present them in book form.

The endnotes to individual chapters mainly serve the purpose of identifying citations in the text, some of which readers might be interested to follow up in detail. The bibliography at the end of the book serves the different purpose of making a few suggestions for further reading.

Henry Mayr-Harting

Contents

LIST OF CONTRIBUTORS

RICHARD HARRIES, Bishop of Oxford, formerly Dean of King's College, London

HENRY MAYR-HARTING, Regius Professor of Ecclesiastical History, University of Oxford

AVERIL CAMERON, Warden of Keble College, Oxford

HENRY CHADWICK, Formerly Dean of Christ Church, Oxford, and Master of Peterhouse, Cambridge

JANE GARNETT, Fellow of Wadham College, Oxford

ADRIAN HASTINGS, Emeritus Professor of Theology, University of Leeds, Diocesan Priest, Masaka, Uganda, 1958–66

DIARMAID MACCULLOCH, Professor of the History of the Church, University of Oxford

ALEXANDER MURRAY, Fellow and Praelector of University College, Oxford

JANE SHAW, Fellow of Regent's Park College, Oxford

KALLISTOS WARE, Bishop of Diokleia, Spalding Lecturer in Eastern Orthodox Studies, University of Oxford

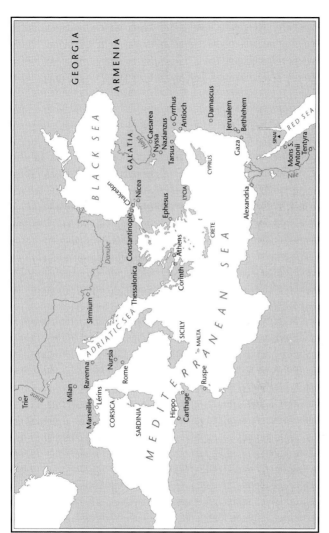

Figure 1. Early Church and Late Antiquity

Figure 2. The Christian West *c.*500–1600

1

THE EARLY CHURCH

Henry Chadwick

Loss of memory is sad. More than we know our lives are influenced by our past. There may of course be things in it that we have no right to forget and wish we could consign to oblivion. In a version of the ancient myth of Hades, not all the dead are allowed to go and drink of the waters of forgetfulness. But here will also be much for which memory is grateful. These lectures attempt to remind us in outline where we have come from in the story of all who have seen and still see in Jesus of Nazareth the most important single event for humanity.

In protest or gratitude our present modern world was itself created by the past whether recent, medieval, or ancient, and we study ancient, medieval, and early modern humanity with tools forged in the present. Consciously or unconsciously our goal is to reach greater understanding of where we are and how on earth we got here. In beginning from the church in ancient society we are looking at the nursery of European civilization. Into this the early church injected faith in a merciful act of God making himself known to a wretched and rebellious race, and through the central person of Jesus of Nazareth, uniquely chosen to be redeemer, continuing this act through a community to communicate to believers forgiveness, renewal, and a high moral discipline.

Ancient society already had the extraordinary achievements of Greek philosophers, mathematicians, and scientists like Archimedes or the brilliant Eratosthenes of Alexandria who with an amazing degree of accuracy measured the diameter of our planet. The Roman conquest of territory from Hadrian's wall to Mesopotamia brought a coherent system of law and administration. Greeks and Romans had an uneasy relationship to one another, and both were initially opposed to the church of Jesus the Christ or Messiah. But there was enough convergence and apparent identity to make the blend work. Stoic ideas of conscience and natural law were congenial to Christians. Tertullian wrote, 'Seneca often writes like one of us'.[1] Epictetus can be very near the New Testament.[2] Platonist philosophers talked of teaching the soul to rise from the beauty and order of this world to another higher realm of heavenly vision. That seemed close to what the Christians aimed to do. The hedonism of Epicurus got him a bad press in antiquity, but Augustine of Hippo judged that he had got a surprising amount right.[3] The old Roman empire fortified its frontiers to keep out barbarian tribesmen. From Constantine the Great imperial policy was to convert them into men of peace, to incorporate groups of them within the empire by a mix of army recruitment and civilizing intention, admittedly with the consequence that in time the barbarians took over the west.

The society which resulted from this blend of Greek, Roman, and Hebraic (and eventually barbarian) took it for granted that decisions rested not so much on an independent individualism but on authority, whether of the church's primary ministers or of the emperor and his prefects. Pre-Christian society had profound respect for what was ancient, even primeval, partly because of the wonderful poetry of Homer which continued to be read until the fall of Con-stantinople to the Turks. Innovation was not an ancient ideal. These features speak of the difference from our modern world where decisions have the frailty of merely human authority, where appeals to reason to provide greater consensus seem effective only when a figleaf for self-interest, and where the sole factors considered concern the empirical world. A week is a long time in politics. The church thought in millennia, and had its eyes looking beyond this world. Its otherworldliness made it potent here and now.

The European character or stamp of Christianity is a legacy of the Roman empire, in which the emperors claimed to be lords of the entire inhabited world.[4] The mission of the church largely began by evangelizing this empire in the face of hostility from emperors and officials. An empire with a world mission found an affinity with a religious group with a kindred aspiration. Several Christians, following a strong hint in Paul's letter to the Romans, believed that in the providence of God the destinies of church and empire were mysteriously linked. This is surprising because the first Christians were Jews, as were Jesus and Paul. In the empire observant Jews enjoyed uneasy tolerance but did not admire Roman lust for domination. Romans met scepticism when they argued that

3

stopping piracy, building roads, and establishing law and order facilitated the unworldly study of the Mosaic law.[5] Jews were numerous in Rome and Egypt, and the dispersion of Jews outside Judaea would be material help to the Christians.

A carpenter's son in Galilee north of Judaea, Jesus called his fellow Jews to religious reform, to a greater inwardness higher than ceremonial rules, to expect the imminent kingdom of God in process of being inaugurated through his gospel, to pursue an ethic higher than observing 613 commands in the law of Moses and elaborations of these by learned rabbis. He soon had a large following, but the larger it became the more alarmed were the powerful ruling class of Sadducees who feared that the imperial governor Pilate might smell sedition and unleash suppression. Judaea already had bands called Zealots determined to liberate Judaea from Roman power. Some Zealots looked to Jesus to be a divinely sent king who would fulfil ancient prophecy and set the Jews free by violence. A fortissimo theme in the Gospels speaks of Jesus' repeated disowning of a militarist Messiahship. Those who took the sword would perish with the sword.

When the emperor Caligula decided to erect his statue in the temple at Jerusalem, all Jews, including those for whom Jesus was Messiah, regarded this as the abomination of desolation standing where he ought not in the very sanctuary of God. Echoes of the horror this caused appear in the New Testament.[6] The Christians were as outraged as any other Jews, no less resenting Roman tyranny and folly.

In St John's Gospel the Highpriest Caiaphas is plausibly seen to persuade the highpriestly council or Sanhedrin that in the interest of public order Pilate the prefect must be urged to execute Jesus before a major uprising provokes a Roman reaction.[7] Paradoxically, though a Roman governor crucifies Jesus, three centuries later the Emperor Constantine is a professing follower of the God of the Christians, and a substantial proportion of his subjects share this belief. Texts as early as the mid-second century look forward to the emperor's conversion.[8] About the year 200 in north Africa Tertullian could be confident that the emperor would want to be Christian if only his duties did not require very secular and un-Christian actions.[9] The Christians themselves were amazed at the rapidity of the church's growth, and the integrity of martyrs under the persecutions caused the reverse effect to that intended. The blood of the martyrs turned out to be a seed.[10] Before the end of the second century educated pagan writers registered alarm at what they called a 'revolution'.[11] The church embodied not merely an alternative culture but a counter-culture. In his personal aphorisms the Emperor Marcus Aurelius, who being a Stoic approved of suicide, complained of the theatrical publicity of Christian martyrs.[12] That publicity was the consequence of the Roman decision to condemn Christians to face hungry wild beasts in the lately built Colosseum or provincial amphitheatres, providing entertainment for crowds of spectators twenty or thirty thousand strong, an astonished audience of huge size for the martyrs' witness. By the third century everybody knew the outlines of Christian belief and believers' willingness to die for their faith.

Judaism already had various schools of thought about the right way to keep the Mosaic law. Besides aristocratic Sadducees there were Pharisees, serious and precise about finer points of ceremony, self-conscious of being distinct from those called the People of the Land. A number of Pharisees were sympathetic to the impassioned seriousness of Jesus' teaching. Saul of Tarsus, hostile at first, was not unique in being a converted Pharisee. After the Romans destroyed Jerusalem in the year 70, temple sacrifices were no longer possible. Conservative Pharisees and Jewish Christians became rivals offering alternative ways of spiritual worship, a rivalry reflected in the 23rd chapter of Matthew's Gospel. Even there the criticism of the Pharisees is that they fail to practise the primary principles of their noble religion. In addition a group by the Dead Sea, probably Essenes, responsible for gathering the Dead Sea Scrolls, had books that throw light on some New Testament writings. From the Jewish matrix Christians inherited a book religion and a tradition of commentaries on that book.

Nevertheless there were two major problems for Jews convinced that Jesus fulfilled prophecy of the coming Messiah or Anointed of God. The first problem was the contrast between a crucified Jesus and nationalist expectation of a soldier-hero destined to expel Roman prefects and their oppressive tax-collectors. This question was answered by observing that, while some prophets expected a national liberator, others such as Isaiah wrote of a suffering servant of the Lord: 'Surely he has borne our griefs and carried our sorrows.' The second lay in a growing conviction that Messiah's coming meant not only, as some said, the imminent end of the world but also an extension of the word of God beyond the boundaries of Judaism into the Gentile world without requiring exact observance of ceremonial Levitical law.

The framework of the earliest Christians' faith was a universalized Judaism from the Hebrew prophets. They believed in the Creator's supreme goodness and transcendent power shown by the power and glory of the natural order. Secondly, that human nature does not now correspond to the Creator's intention but is flawed by disobedience; thirdly, that the coming of redemption in Jesus the Christ is not an isolated divine act but continues a providential care manifest in Moses and the Hebrew prophets; fourthly, that by his eternal Spirit the Lord is still present with his people; fifthly, he has given pledges of his mercy and love in covenant signs, namely baptism in water and the memorial sacrifice or great thanksgiving which the ancient Gentile Christians called *Eucharistia*. This last rite, to which his presence and offering are central themes, was and is a source of healing and renewal to the baptized. Those under instruction, called catechumens, were allowed to attend the first part of the service, psalm, readings, sermon, but then left. These two covenant signs Latin theology a millennium later defined with the term 'sacrament', meaning a physical act carrying meaning and effect for mind and soul. Greek churches were content with the term 'mysteries'.

There were already Gentiles impressed by the high ethic of Jewish families, wanting to be associated with a universal monotheism rather than the mainly local cults of heathen society. Some pagan thinkers criticized the placating of gods by animal sacrifices, which (some said) were bribery for inferior gods who liked that kind of thing, not fitting for high brass like Zeus or Jupiter.[13] Synagogues even in Judaea and Galilee could have a few God-fearing Gentiles attending their worship and hearing the Old Testament read and expounded. The Gospels record one Roman centurion who paid for the building of a synagogue. But it was rare for a Gentile attending sabbath services to be circumcised or to feel obliged not to eat pork. To the early Christian mission it seemed natural to recruit such adherents, and this could not please observant Jews resistant to assimilation. Resentment and anger were inevitable and produced attacks. Moreover at the time of the Jewish revolts in 66–70, 116, and especially in 133–5, Christian Jews stood aside from the Zealot struggle, and this engendered some ferocity of reaction.

A feature of Jewish communities was and is care for widows and orphans, the poor and weak. This passed to the church; Tertullian could quote pagans saying, 'See how these Christians love one another.'[14] Two prominent critics of Christianity, Porphyry and the emperor Julian, tried unsuccessfully to get pagan religion to operate a welfare system on this model. Unlike the Jews, the Christians upset Roman authorities by an aversion to capital punishment, initially in all circumstances. This disqualified at least some of them from being magistrates or provincial governors and at first from the army. The government did not see how society could defend itself without force of law and sanctions. By 200 there were Christian magistrates, by 300 Christian governors of provinces, specially excused participation in pagan sacrifices.[15] It is fair to add that some pagan governors felt glad if they did not have to execute anyone during their term of office.[16]

Roman pagans were accustomed to Jews staying away from the cults of the gods; one second-century Platonist, Celsus, remarked, 'their religion seems very peculiar but is at least that of their ancestors' which makes it tolerable.[17] The Christians, however, were going to be drawn from any and every ethnic group and their critical rejection of the old gods was offensive. The gods of Rome might have childish and superstitious ceremonies, but they were believed to have bestowed a world empire on the city of Rome. The army invoked their aid to defend frontiers against barbarian invasion. Rich merchants prayed for success in commerce. People resorted to them with amulets, for healing, for fertile wives and crops, for safe travel, for success in love. We hear of wealthy senators without belief in the gods who guided their lives by consulting astrologers.[18]

It is ironical perhaps that the Christians did not know that that is what they were until pagan outsiders gave them this name. Pagans had no collective noun to describe them until from the third century Latin Christians said *pagani*, a word either for country folk or colloquial soldiers' jargon for non-combatants. Early Christianity was urban long before it penetrated the conservative countryside. On the other hand, baptism was enrolment to serve as a soldier of Christ. So either derivation is possible, the non-combatant sense more probable. In the Greek east Christians continued with the Jews' term 'Hellenes' (cf. Acts 21: 28).

By *paganitas* or *paganismus* (both forms occur),[19] Christians meant worship of material objects made by human hands, belief in astral determinism and horoscopes, and resort to soothsayers for predicting the future. There long continued people close to or within the church who resorted to the old gods for healings and to fortune-tellers and sorcerers, especially if they had a sick child.

The Apostle Paul as apostle to the Gentiles needed a

justification for abandoning the Mosaic law, and formulated the admittedly intricate doctrine of justification by faith, not by keeping the Levitical law. This strengthened the break between church and synagogue. The Christians naturally took over Passover and Pentecost re-interpreted as the passion of Christ and as the gift of the Holy Spirit. A crucial shift from Judaism was to meet for worship on the first day of the week, our Sunday, rather than on the Sabbath.[20] This was the day of the Lord's resurrection; this was the day when Paul's missionary congregations worshipped. The words 'Abba' (Father), especially 'Amen', and 'Alleluia' continued in Gentile Christian Liturgy. Beside the Eucharist the Christians had an occasional love-feast or *agápe*, at which a wealthy member provided hospitality for the entire congregation, many of whom were poor and hungry.[21] If the host allowed, they could take food away in their pockets called a 'take-away' (*apophoreton*, the first doggy bag).[22] One ancient papyrus records a love-feast paid for by a friendly pagan soldier grateful for Christian kindness.[23] In Egypt one immensely influential man was converted by the kindness of a local Christian community to his military unit (Pachomius). It became customary for bishops to provide a communal meal on the anniversary of their consecration, called *natalis* or birthday.[24]

In Gentile churches there was debate about the continued reading of the Old Testament. Soon some claimed that there are two gods: the God of the Old Testament was no more than just, while the God of Jesus was love and goodness. Gnostics believed that the Creator was either malevolent or incompetent and could not be the supreme power and goodness. The apostle Paul of Tarsus had begun as a vehement conservative and observant Pharisee out to suppress the Christian mission to the Gentiles, but by a vision of the risen Lord was converted to belief that it was indeed right, and that he was called to be its advocate with the defensively conservative Christian Pharisees at Jerusalem. Peaceful coexistence was going to be difficult for both sides. He saw the Mosaic law as delivering one safely to Christ's school.[25]

There is no more Jewish Christian book in the New Testament than the Revelation of John of Patmos with its mosaic of Old Testament quotations. Not all churches accepted this book into their lectionary. There was also disagreement in the early church about John's vision of an angel imprisoning the Devil for a thousand years or the expectation of Christ returning to a rebuilt Jerusalem to reign with saints for a millennium.

Fervent hope of an imminent and, for all but the elect, terrifying end to the world was discouraged by Hippolytus in a commentary on Daniel. Origen and later Augustine of Hippo held the millennium to be an allegorical or mythological concept. (The coming of the first millennium was feared by some with foreboding.)

Before Christian times, there were people under Zoroastrian influence calculating when the world would end. Political crises stimulated this. The fall of Constantinople to the Turks was taken by the then patriarch of Constantinople to be a warning of an imminent end to civilization as he knew it; he carefully calculated that this would occur after his time in Columbus' year AD 1492.[26]

The success of Paul's Gentile mission brought the church

out into a society with many educated people and some trained in philosophy. The strength of Greek culture lay supremely in the mastery of logic, mathematics, and natural science. For Aristotle, an amazing pioneer who got about 80 per cent of it right, the life of the mind is the route to the highest of which humanity is capable. The Roman world was more concerned with government, law, and the preservation of peace when in their interest, and except for Cicero and Seneca philosophy was not their métier.

If there was some natural catastrophe like a drought or earthquake, or a military defeat, the Christians found themselves blamed. Surely the gods were angry at being neglected or scorned. Persecutions of the church in the mid-third century and again early in the fourth under the emperor Diocletian were short and very sharp, mainly because torturers were instructed not to kill their victims but to break down their resistance by recurrent inflictions of physical agony. Tortures at noon every Tuesday exploit the dread of the next instalment. We shall not be censorious of the many who gave way. The churches of the fourth and fifth centuries proudly commemorated their heroes, noble intercessors for their fellow Christians on earth; Augustine once observes that among them there were more women than men.[27]

For the apostle Paul, belief in one God was what made it impossible to think that the knowledge of God and the moral law could be confined to one race alone. The Gentiles, he wrote, know what is right and wrong from their conscience without the law of Moses to guide them.[28] The Christians saw the right and the good as being pre-eminent over the pursuit of power, honour, wealth, and sexual satisfaction. Indeed they came to distinguish a basic or necessary ethic of obedience to divine precepts from a higher dedication which would forgo natural goods. God has made us male and female, so marriage is a great good; but for a higher end to remain unmarried can be a calling for some individuals such as missionaries or pastors.[29]

Ascetics are less prominent in Christian history than in other world religions. Monks and nuns did not come to live a common life in separate communities until the time of Constantine the Great. In his time an illiterate Copt first created a community, with a wise rule about seniority which has been retained by Oxford and Cambridge colleges, namely that a don's seniority dates from the day of admission and nothing else. (His name was Pachomius.) The system happily avoided social difficulty when grandees disillusioned with the world asked for admission. Before communities existed, even in the apostolic age there were local churches with small groups of ascetics. From the third century we first hear of tension between ascetics and the urban-based bishop and parish clergy.[30] This would last.

The monastic movement of the fourth century had numerous critics deeply unsympathetic to the weakening of urban congregations by removing very devout members. Especially in Spain and Gaul the ascetics met a reaction which did not admire what was happening.[31] Jerome once tells us that a common topic of conversation among monks was disparagement of the urban clergy and laity. The alienation was mutual. It became important for bishops to exempt themselves from criticism by being unmarried or, if married, by asking their wives to retire to nunneries or other retreats. Not all wives liked that. One bishop was woken at midnight by his wife hammering on the front door of his house. She was admitted to his bed, and nine months later presented him with a daughter.[32] During the last quarter of the fourth century the then Pope Siricius found that in Gaul there was faction between the two parties for and against clerical celibacy. He sided with supporters of celibacy, but regretted that his ruling had often been ignored.[33] The counter-arguments were that priests in the Old Testament were free to marry and St Paul had been emphatic that marriage is no sin.

Another question for monasteries was economic. In Egypt monasteries founded by Pachomius in the Nile valley near Dendera (Tentyra) provided not only housing but farm labour for numerous unemployed peasants. The mother house had some 3,000 monks. They prospered and there was a dramatic crisis when one of the daughter houses decided to go it alone because it was making money. The religious houses solved the problem of finding a home for girls who had not found a husband. Parents with very modest means used to put their daughters into a nunnery, which provided shelter, food, and simple clothing.[34] But our sources tell us that there were difficulties with women who had no real sense of vocation for the religious life, some of whom secretly took to the bottle.[35] For the impecunious it was not easy to feed and clothe a spinster daughter. Poor parents often solved the economic problem by exposing an infant daughter. Ben Sirach had observed (22: 3) that 'the birth of a daughter means loss'. In north Africa Augustine of Hippo organized nuns to rescue foundlings.[36] We do not know how these foundlings got on as they grew up. One fears that, as in later centuries, even rescued foundlings did not flourish. The expectation of life in antiquity was not great.

A monastery or nunnery soon acquired an enclosing wall to control entrances and exits. To be expelled for obstinate delinquency was a terrifying experience. When a monk died, the coffin was carried to the monastery graveyard with a solemn procession singing psalms,[37] unless it was a case of suicide, when the procession walked in absolute silence and no prayers were said at the graveside. Barbarian raids sometimes carried off monks to sell in the town slave-markets. With a good master in a good house a domestic slave was far better off than a free day-wage labourer.[38] There were Christians such as Gregory of Nyssa who denounced the entire system of servitude,[39] but the plight of many who were free and unemployed was destitution. Augustine was the first to advocate welfare based on redistributing income because of the inadequacy of private almsgiving.

The monk's martyr-spirit of No Compromise emerges at another point—in the concept of standing firm for the true tradition against heresy, that is to say, adherence to opinions which the community at large cannot share because they seem to threaten the lifeline of salvation. It was axiomatic that only fully divine action could redeem poor mortals, living only brief lives, their reason pulled apart by passion and prejudice, their will-power weak, and their love for the right and the good even weaker. Therefore the church was resistant to those who saw in Jesus a wise teacher and inspired prophet but less than the presence of God for us and for our salvation. On the other side there was also resistance to those who, like people combated by Ignatius, held Christ to be so wholly divine that his humanity was only a façade. In the second century, for example, some thought that Jesus ate and drank not because he needed to, but only to forestall heretics who denied it.[40] In short, the heresies that most disturbed ancient Christianity were either doctrines that denied the reality and spontaneity of the humanity of Jesus or those which threatened the possibility of redemption by denying the presence of God in his life, passion, and resurrection. Before long, there were gnostic or Manichee heretics who sharply distinguished a predestinate body of shining elect from the soggy mass of corrupt humanity for whom no hope could be entertained. There would come a necessity of affirming that no one is beyond redemption point but also that every one of us is in need of being redeemed. This became an issue between the great Augustine and the earliest surviving British writer, Pelagius.

Arguments about the definition of orthodoxy or heresy became intricate as contending parties resorted to finer points of logic to defend their case. Augustine once remarks that an exact definition of heresy is virtually impossible.[41] The mutually destructive arguments of the classical schools of Greek philosophy encountered the cynical criticism (Lucian of Samosata) that each was correct in diagnosis of the opposition's errors. By the fourth and fifth centuries the contentions of an earlier millennium had been succeeded by uncomfortable quarrels about the correct and precise formulation of true doctrine. After Boethius had made the logic of Aristotle available to the Latin west, this legacy would come to dominate the medieval schoolmen to an excess which one can see in William of Ockham's commentary on the fourth book of Peter Lombard, discussing the logic of affirmations of eucharistic change. The one thing you would never guess from this brilliant education in logic is that all this had something to do with the sacrament of our redemption. Something of the same reaction is provoked by sixth-century debates between clever partisans about Christology.

This situation was especially apparent in the age after Constantine the Great. Frequent councils of bishops issued differing statements of belief, the effect of which was to weaken the respect in which councils were held. Synods could make mistakes. In the east they retained high teaching authority. For the Latin west, which was less involved than the Greek east, this confidence in synods was not shared, which had the effect of enhancing the already much respected authority of the Roman see. In the east the bishop of Byzantium on the Bosporus, which Constantine had refounded under the title New Rome, commonly called Constantinople, similarly acquired powers which vexed older bishoprics at Alexandria and Syrian Antioch. Both old and new Rome became in time major organs of missionary endeavour in west and east respectively. Rome sent missions to Germany and Britain, Constantinople to the Slav world. At the same time bishops of Constantinople, from the fifth century called patriarchs, had emperors living only a few yards away, too close for comfort. It was harder for them to do what some bishops of old Rome attempted with some success, to protect local bishops and their churches from domination by secular potentates. As the western half of the empire disintegrated into barbarian kingdoms, the Roman see would become a natural focus of coherence and togetherness, and for some centuries to come remained so for the east as well as the west.

An important bishopric which had no secular power was that of Jerusalem, from the fourth century a magnet for pilgrims. Zion the mother of all churches became a liturgical model, and in the Jordan valley and Judaean desert monasteries sprang up in some quantity.[42]

The Christian emperors forged an alliance with the church. In Ambrose of Milan the church can demand that a Christian emperor does not order indiscriminate massacre in retribution for the murder of an army general, and will come as a penitent when that has happened.[43] The church is becoming a determinant factor in a wider civilization. In Jerome and Augustine the church possessed two of the most learned and able minds of their age. So the church became the transmitter of ancient culture. As laity became better educated, they would come to resent clerical power. Add to that the heady wine of nationalism and you get Gallicanism, and then the Reformation.

During the fourth, fifth, and sixth centuries we see symptoms of occasional alienation between Greek east and Latin west. The west had been pleased by the first ecumenical council at Nicaea (Iznik) in 325, but was profoundly annoyed by the canons of the second council at Constantinople in 381, as was also the bishop of Alexandria. When twenty-five years later John Chrysostom, bishop of Constantinople and a noble confessor for the cause of the poor and oppressed, lost the support of the imperial court and was deposed by a synod, Bishop Innocent I of Rome protested, and asked the eastern patriarchs to insert John's name among the saints with whom their church was in communion. For many years the Roman request was ignored. Political relations between Constantinople and the western emperor at Ravenna were already bad, and the affair of John did not help. The seeds of alienation between Latin west and Greek east were sown in this period, Greeks thinking of church authority in conciliar terms, Latins in primatial language of jurisdiction.

Many books tell us that the split between eastern and western churches occurred in the year 1054. It is of course not so simple. Three decades later the Pope, Urban II, was asking the emperor at Constantinople if there had been a schism of some sort that no one had mentioned to him.

When east and west came to the parting of the ways is not a datable event. Ecclesial bodies cease to be in communion with one another when they think they are. But if you have asked yourself why Russians and Greeks have supported the Serbs in the affair of Kosovo, the evident answer is that peoples with a religious adherence to or a past history of eastern Orthodoxy, easily think of the Latin west as likely to be wrong. That has its roots in the post-Constantinian church.

The history of the Christian church is one of controversy, not infrequently toughly argued because of the ideals and highmindedness of the parties. The apostolic age was one of great diversity, which was gradually standardized during the period under review here. The churches of the second century found coherence and stability by the communion of bishops. By the last two decades of the second century they had an authoritative collection of books closely resembling our New Testament and were developing the interpretation of the Old Testament. Gradually the expression of the Christian story of

God the Father, the incarnation of the Son, and the Holy Spirit immanent in the life of the church, in Bible and sacraments, was expressed in shared affirmations of faith that we call creeds. The fascination of ancient church history is that we see Christianity deciding to take the form in which we now recognize it.

2

LATE ANTIQUITY

Averil Cameron

The period covered in this chapter has often been portrayed either as the golden age of early Christianity, or as a time when it was corrupted from its early purity by association with the state. Each of these views is an over-simplification, the second perhaps more so, with its implication of an Ur-faith, existing pure and undefiled from the beginning, and its moral and religious idealization of the first Christians. Contemporary discussion of the relation of church and state in our own society, however, also makes the questions raised in this lecture particularly relevant to the modern world.

The term 'late antiquity' is not an altogether innocent one, and we must try to define it further. In the first place, the term 'late antiquity'—rather than, say, 'the later Roman empire'—avoids the older concepts of 'decline and fall'. In current usage, it denotes more or less the period from, say, Constantine, to the rise of Islam, and it applies to the whole sweep of the Mediterranean, both east and west. It allows us to take almost a postmodern panoramic view of a multicultural, polyglot world, which includes Syriac, Coptic, Georgian, and Armenian speakers in the east, and Celts, Gauls, and Germans in the west. It helps at least to some extent to break down the connotation of triumphalism so often associated with the growth of Christianity in the Roman state. Indeed, as I shall go on to argue, various forms of paganism remained lively and persistent in many parts of this world, even at the end of the period. Yet this was indeed the time when Christianity took such solid root that it ultimately became the religion of Europe and of Byzantium. The challenge for a historian therefore is to explain how that came about, but to do so without resorting to triumphalist assumptions and while still retaining a sense of balance.

In the definition that I have adopted, late antiquity begins in the later third century AD and continues until at least the sixth century, the reign of the Emperor Justinian (AD 527–65) and after. With the Islamic conquests of the early seventh century, a new era dawned, bringing with it the loss of nearly a third of all the territory of the Byzantine empire, very largely in the eastern provinces. Not only the religious map of the Mediterranean, but also its social and economic configuration were redrawn. The real beginning of the medieval world, therefore, may well be put somewhere in the early seventh century (which is not to deny that profound changes had already taken place in the west before this date). However, I shall concentrate in this chapter especially on the fourth and early fifth centuries, the period that saw the reign of Constantine the Great (who died in 337), the flowering of the institutional church, the rise of monasticism, and many of the greatest figures of the patristic age, men like Athanasius of Alexandria, Basil of Caesarea, Ambrose of Milan, the two Gregorys, Gregory of Nazianzus and Gregory of Nyssa, and John Chrysostom—each one of them at one and the same time bishop, theologian, writer, and ascetic.

The position of Christianity in the Roman empire at the end of the fourth century AD was very different from how things had been a century earlier, at the end of the third. At the end of the third century, Christians were still a very small minority indeed—estimates vary from 10 per cent down to as low as 2 per cent. They were concentrated especially in cities, particularly eastern, Greek-speaking cities. There were churches, but not the great public basilicas of later times. There were of course major Christian writers and scholars, such as Cyprian, bishop of Carthage (later martyred), and the great theologian Origen of Caesarea in Palestine (died *c.*254), who commented on books of the Bible and laid the foundations for the biblical scholarship of Eusebius and Jerome. But powerful voices were also raised in hostility and opposition to the faith. For example, the pagan writer Porphyry wrote an important work in the later third century attacking Christianity, to whose refutation Eusebius of Caesarea devoted much time and effort. It was quite possible at this stage that Porphyry's views might have prevailed. He argued for the primacy of Greek philosophy and the efficacy of oracles and oracular shrines such as the great temple of Apollo at Delphi, and Eusebius of Caesarea had to argue extremely hard to persuade his readers that pagan oracles were in fact false, and that the temples were, as he put it, the homes only of dead idols and demons. In fact the great oracular shrines of Greece and Asia

Minor were still in full swing, as we know from plentiful epigraphic evidence. There was much hostility to Christianity, and in AD 303 the pagan emperors of the early years of the fourth century thought it worthwhile to launch a counter-offensive in the form of a renewed persecution. This time clergy were particularly affected, especially in the eastern provinces, and even if there were not as many gruesome deaths as later martyrologies claimed, a good number were tortured and incarcerated. Survivors of this treatment, with their scars and mutilated limbs, were a notable sight at the Council of Nicaea called by Constantine in AD 325.

A century or so later things looked very different. In the early 390s, the Emperor Theodosius I passed a series of laws which made paganism illegal, and in a further step, subjected heretics to the punishments of the law. Such was the power of some Christian bishops that the same emperor was humbled and made to do penance by Ambrose, bishop of Milan (*c.*339–97), even if in contrast John Chrysostom, less clever in his dealings with the imperial court, was deposed from his episcopal see in Constantinople on two separate occasions. The emperor's household in Constantinople in the mid-fifth century was held by some to resemble a religious house. Most major cities had by now acquired impressive and expensive churches, which were beginning to be decorated with religious pictures—scenes from the Old and New Testaments, there, as some saw it, for the edification of the uneducated. One of the earliest surviving apse mosaics, showing Christ and the apostles against a background of Christian Jerusalem, is in the church of S. Pudenziana in Rome and dates from about 390. Other spectacularly decorated churches soon followed, among them S. Maria Maggiore in Rome, built by Sixtus III in the 430s, with one of the earliest formal depictions of the Virgin Mary, dressed like a Roman empress. The Ravenna churches of S. Apollinare Nuovo, S. Apollinare in Classe and San Vitale belong to the sixth century, the latter, with its famous mosaics of the emperor and empress Justinian and Theodora in liturgical procession, erected by the local bishop in 547.

As the church took on a more public role, questions of unity also became more and more pressing, and by the late fourth century two major ecumenical councils had been held, at Nicaea (AD 325) and Constantinople (AD 381), as well as many minor ones; two more great councils, at Ephesus (AD 431) and Chalcedon (AD 451), were to follow in the fifth century. Dissent was labelled as heresy and if necessary punished by the state, but this happened against a background of intense religious controversy, expressed in theological writings and in local synods whose status was often vigorously challenged. Finally bishops had acquired great influence; they often controlled considerable wealth and property, they acquired jurisdiction and they had the ear of governors and emperors, whom they not infrequently challenged.

Whatever its real motivation may have been, the decision of Constantine to favour the Christian church after his victory over Maxentius in the battle of the Milvian Bridge in AD 312 was at the very heart of these changes. Perhaps, though, his decision was in fact not so very surprising. There were Christians in high places in the courts both of Constantine and of his colleagues and rivals, and he was not the only imperial aspirant to show favour to them. But Constantine

ruthlessly eliminated his rivals, including the pro-Christian
Licinius, and persisted in his support of the church even when
he found to his chagrin that Christians were divided bitterly
among each other. Something sparked off in him a real
engagement, such that he joined in their disputes himself.
Already at a very early stage he claimed that God had set him
the task of establishing right religion in the empire, and he
took this seriously enough to expect divine punishment
should he fail.[1] The emperor also ventured into composing
Christian apologetic himself, writing a lengthy speech known
as the *Oration to the Saints* in which he set out the framework of
Christian salvation. He was followed as an active theologian
by several later emperors, of whom Justinian was one of the
most enthusiastic, but Constantine took it a step further and
preached weekly sermons to his reluctant courtiers.

Leaving aside the question of his personal commitment,
perhaps the two most important results of Constantine's
policy were his initiative in calling a worldwide council to
settle matters of faith, funded from state resources; and the
structural change he brought about by enhancing the status of
bishops, allowing the church to inherit property and wealth,
and giving tax and other reliefs to clergy. His own example of
church building in Rome, in and around Jerusalem, where he
himself ordered the building of a great basilica on the site of
the tomb of Christ, and to a lesser extent at Constantinople
and Antioch, set a pattern for the patronage of the church by
the rich and for its growing wealth. He also found eager
supporters among the bishops. Only a very few maintained
their doctrinal resistance at the Council of Nicaea. The rest,
like his panegyrist Eusebius of Caesarea, who had gone to the

Council under formal condemnation by a synod held at Antioch, and who had promised his congregation to maintain their doctrinal views at the Council, were overcome by the wonder of an emperor who was on their side, and signed up to the credal formula in which Constantine was claimed to have had a major role.

The creed of Nicaea was not the only matter debated by the Council, which was also much concerned with differences in practice within the church over the date of Easter. But it is the one for which it was most remembered and which was to have momentous repercussions in Christian history. The extent of disagreement is glossed over by Eusebius, who describes instead the imperial banquet to which the bishops were invited after the Council, which seemed to him like the sight of Christ reigning in heaven.[2] He and others had their own agendas when claiming imperial support, and Eusebius later worked out a theory of church and state which placed the emperor on earth in a relationship of imitation to God in heaven, and defined his major duty as that of establishing piety to God within his domain. But this philosophy, so congenial to bishops like Eusebius, was soon shown to be over-simplified, when even within Constantine's own lifetime the settlement achieved at the Council of Nicaea failed to endure. After only ten years had passed, Constantine agreed to the exile of Athanasius of Alexandria, the great defender of Nicaea, who had attended the Council as a deacon, and matters changed still more after Constantine died, when his three sons failed to achieve concord and turned on each other, having already authorized a wholesale massacre of rival members of the imperial family. One of their first acts on being made Augusti was to recall exiled bishops, including Athanasius, but this was a political gesture far from being a sign of future reconciliation, and the reign of Constantine's son Constantius II (d. 361) was characterized by an ongoing struggle between Athanasius and the secular power represented by the emperor.

Constantine found in the church a potential second administrative structure, which mimicked the imperial one, and only required a head for its hierarchy. It was a natural move, but a momentous one, for him to extend to Christian clergy the same privileges that were customary for pagan priests, and to expect provincial governors to make their resources available to allow bishops to attend church councils. According to Eusebius, the emperor treated bishops with great deference and they were given powers of jurisdiction in the courts. Since the church was now legally able to own and inherit property, individual bishops soon found themselves controlling and administering substantial funds. How they used these sums in the light of the conflicting demands of Christian charity and of the natural desire to build churches and related buildings, which would promote their see and immortalize themselves, is a major theme of the ensuing period. However, Constantine's position *vis-à-vis* the bishops was complex. He did not (and no doubt could not) establish himself as head of the church, preferring to describe himself as the 'bishop of those outside'.[3] Yet neither was there a clearcut hierarchy among the major sees. The question of authority was therefore left unsettled, and this ambiguity left many problems for later emperors as they tried to bring about church unity. The issues quickly became clear to Constantine as he realized the range of opinions on matters of doctrine and the real differences of practice between one part of the empire and the other. It was no easier for his son and successor Constantius II, or indeed, for the emperors of the fifth and sixth centuries. Unity was established as a constant aim, both for religious and for political reasons; but one emperor after another was to find it elusive.

One clear result of the initiatives of Constantine was, however, the establishment of the concept of a Christian Holy Land, and with it the growth of pilgrimage to the holy places. Constantine's church of the Holy Sepulchre in Jerusalem was built over what was believed to be the site of the burial and resurrection of Jesus. It symbolized the end of the pagan era represented by the establishment of the Roman colony of Aelia Capitolina after the fall of Jerusalem, and by ostentatiously leaving the Jewish Temple in ruins it proclaimed the new Jerusalem as a Christian city. Pilgrims soon followed in numbers, including Egeria, a Spanish nun who visited the biblical sites in the 380s and left a diary of her experiences which contains our best evidence for the liturgy as practised in Jerusalem.[4] The local economy prospered and pilgrimage became big business, not only in Palestine but at other Christian centres such as the great shrine of Thecla in Asia Minor. This led inevitably to 'discoveries' of the relics of saints and martyrs, the greatest of which was of course the relic of the True Cross, whose discovery was by the end of the fourth century and later universally attributed to Constantine's mother Helena. As now, pilgrims wanted souvenirs, and thousands of such tokens have survived, notably small plaques, and earthenware bottles stamped with Christian designs, which would have held a little of the soil of the Holy Land. Pagans travelled on pilgrimages too; but from now on Christians outdid them in enthusiasm and sheer numbers.

They travelled not just to the holy places associated with the life of Jesus, but to the sites connected with Christian saints—holy men and women—or indeed to visit the monks themselves in their monasteries and cells in the Egyptian or Syrian desert. By the end of the fourth century visiting the monks in Egypt had become so much a pastime for aristocratic Christians from Rome and elsewhere, men and women alike, that the theme of further withdrawal becomes a common one in the monastic literature. As we can also see from the classic *Life of Antony*, written soon after Antony's death in the 350s,[5] the monastic ideal did not envisage total withdrawal on a permanent basis; it also required the anchorite to be available for advice and for the giving of hospitality to strangers. Paradoxically, perhaps, to those accustomed to the later western monastic tradition, monks in this period sometimes played an active role in political disputes, and could prove a disruptive influence as well as a quietist one. The so-called Tall Brothers are a good example, as they brought their influence to bear in disputes in Constantinople at the end of the fourth century. There was no single model for the religious life. Basil of Caesarea is often credited with laying down the pattern for orthodox monasticism. Yet it was also common for individuals, especially women, to lead dedicated religious lives within their own domestic environment, which might well be in a town or city; others, again, adopted more extreme lifestyles altogether, like the Syrian female ascetics recorded by Theodoret, the fifth-century bishop of Cyrrhus in northern Syria, who lived chained up in a cowshed,[6] or the stylite saints who were claimed to have spent years on end standing upright on the tops of pillars, where they were sometimes visited by important—even imperial—personages.

'Where did all this madness come from?' E. R. Dodds asked about asceticism in the fine book of his Wiles Lectures, *Pagan and Christian in an Age of Anxiety* (Cambridge, 1963), p. 34. He confessed that he did not know, and as a good rationalist he attributed the success of Christianity to the sense of community it gave to isolated people in the Roman world. Nowadays we might look to other kinds of explanations, including for instance the development of new styles of communication. But I think we should also recognize in these movements in late antiquity the shock of the new, the enthusiasm of individuals realizing that they were in a world of new possibilities. Old barriers had come down; anything was possible. A generation which has seen the fall of the Berlin Wall should not underestimate the amazement with which Christians like Eusebius witnessed the ending of persecution and the dawn of imperial favour. For some at least, the religious life represented an escape and a new excitement. Perhaps this was most true of the aristocrats who took to asceticism with such enthusiasm. High-born Roman ladies dressed in the clothes of the poor, became groupies of St Jerome, learned Hebrew and went off to the Holy Land to found monasteries, enrol on the register of the poor in Jerusalem or visit the monks of Egypt. Mixed motives abounded. Jerome was hounded out of Rome for persuading the daughters of the senatorial class to starve themselves into anorexia. But his loyal female friends followed him to his monastery at Bethlehem and set up chaste establishments nearby so that they could continue their elevated and pious conversations. The Greek *Life of Antony*, translated into Latin at Jerome's instigation, was taken up by bright young civil servants at the imperial court at Milan, from whom Augustine heard of it.[7] Part of the reason for Christian enthusiasm among well-born women may have arisen from the simple fact that spare daughters were a burden to an aristocratic family in this society, though on the other hand noble Roman families did not want marriageable daughters running off to become dedicated virgins. But it was not just the daughters who were attracted.

This was still the ancient world, and there was no media revolution. But in thinking about the fourth century one is struck by the vivacity of Christian communication systems. Letter-writing for one thing; most bishops were great letter-writers, to each other, to lay persons, to provincial governors and to members of the imperial elite. The sheer number of letters which survive is amazing enough. They are letters of patronage, letters of spiritual direction, letters of advice. Augustine was a major letter-writer, though once he became a bishop of Hippo on the coast of North Africa he never again left the province; instead, when letters were not enough, people came to him, especially when Rome was taken by the Visigoths in 410. Somehow people also knew where to go on pilgrimage, what were the best routes and the best sites to choose. All the great Fathers of the fourth century were voluminous writers—volumes and volumes of letters, sermons, commentaries, treatises. Why did they write so much?

Even if we suppose that few will have read them, they thought it worth while to write all these works.

As the fourth century wears on, we find Christian bishops taking the high ground. Ambrose of Milan pronounced the funeral oration for the Emperor Theodosius I; Gregory of Nazianzus, one of the three great Cappadocian fathers, was generally reckoned to be the best Greek orator since Demosthenes. His friend Basil of Caesarea had been a star student in what was effectively the University of Athens. As bishop of Constantinople at the end of the fourth century, John Chrysostom held congregations in thrall week by week, and became embroiled in the bitter quarrels of city factions and the imperial family. Most of these men had been trained in exactly the same way as pagan rhetors and teachers of higher education, and alongside them. Augustine had been a teacher of rhetoric himself, and it shows in his writings. In a remarkably modern way (but it is the experience of a teacher showing through) he knew how to hold an audience, and how to reach people of different educational levels. Men like Jerome felt that they had to excuse the simple language in which the New Testament was written ('the language of fishermen'), but did not hesitate themselves to use all the tricks of the best education the fourth century could offer. Some of this spread to their acolytes, and some of Jerome's women friends are credited with toiling through thousands of lines of Hebrew.

It was an age when Christianity became the subject of a refined scholarship which can seem somewhat surprising to modern taste. When Bishop Epiphanius of Salamis in Cyprus wrote a learned treatise in which he classified eighty dangerous heresies, he chose the number because there were eighty concubines in the Song of Songs. Every respectable church Father of the fourth century wrote a long commentary on the opening chapters of the Book of Genesis. In part this was to reaffirm the biblical doctrine of creation, but it was also needed in order to explain the more difficult aspects of the biblical narrative. The pagan view that the world had had no beginning needed to be answered, and Christians therefore welcomed Plato's *Timaeus*, where a creation myth could be found. But the opening chapters of Genesis were also critically important to Christians for other reasons: for explaining sexual difference, or for justifying asceticism ('were Adam and Eve sexual beings in the Garden of Eden?', was a question often asked). They were equally vital for combating astrology and fatalism, the belief that the heavenly bodies conditioned human lives—a persistent idea very much alive today and which the Fathers were very anxious to refute. God had created the heavenly bodies, they repeated, and they were no more and no less than part of his creation.

The Bible presented a tremendous challenge to Christian writers of this period, and the Old Testament was not always easy to explain. It was often inconsistent and for Christians it did not always prefigure the New in a clear manner. All the major Fathers of this period were therefore also biblical scholars, in the sense that they struggled in different ways to make sense of the biblical text. The Book of Genesis was not the only problem, but it was one of the most central ones: Basil of Caesarea wrote on the *Hexaemeron*, the six days of creation; John Chrysostom wrote numerous sermons on

Genesis; Augustine wrestled with it and returned to it over and over again during his lifetime. One of his attempts to explicate it is entitled 'On the literal interpretation of Genesis'; should one understand such a text literally or perhaps figuratively? Such dilemmas lay behind all the exegesis of the period, and it is not surprising that there should have been major disagreements in approach.

It is hard to convey the sheer volume of writings, and the energy of their authors. It is nothing to have literally hundreds of surviving letters and dozens of sermons and treatises from each major author, and the number of surviving manuscripts containing works by John Chrysostom itself runs into the thousands. These writings were also extremely varied in kind; Basil of Caesarea for example wrote sermons, treatises, and ascetic works, including prescriptions for the religious life. We should remember again that nearly all the Fathers of this period had received an excellent secular education, which equipped them extremely well for their writing project. Basil had been a fellow-pupil of Libanius at Athens. These are the intellectuals of the church and the church leaders of their generation, and one of the things that they were doing was quite simply to develop a specifically Christian learning and a public Christian rhetoric—no small achievement for a faith which still in some people's eyes rested on its appeal to the uneducated—women and slaves in the eyes of the pagan Celsus. But the status of Christian knowledge raised funda-mental issues about the nature of truth, and typically, it was Augustine more than anyone, a professional teacher himself, who saw the paradox and the contradiction between the inspired word of God and worldly learning, and Augustine who composed a treatise on Christian learning. His own involvement with secular Latin literature was long and complex, but ultimately the only source of true learning must be God alone.

It is a great mistake to suppose that paganism, or polytheism, as some modern scholars prefer to call it, was dead or dying by the end of the fourth century. Take the great oracles, for example. Eusebius of Caesarea would have us believe that they were silent: the gods had been defeated by their Christian rival and no longer spoke from Didyma, Delphi, or Claros. In fact we know that the oracular shrines continued to operate and continued to be visited. At the other end of the scale, sixth-century country bishops like Nicholas of Sion in Lycia had to contend with the survival of practices such as tree worship. When John of Ephesus was sent out by Justinian on a mission to convert pagans in Asia Minor in a similar period he claimed no less than 70,000 souls. At times Christians resorted to violence in their attacks on pagans, which suggests that paganism was very much still a threat. One such incident was the destruction of the great temple of Serapis in Alexandria in 391; another was the lynching by Christians of the female philosopher Hypatia in the same city in 415; yet another was the destruction of the temple of Zeus Marnas at Gaza with the aid of imperial troops called in by the local bishop in 402. These are isolated incidents, perhaps, but they tell us just how urgent the struggle actually was.

The effort to distinguish Christianity clearly from Judaism also remained on the agenda. Recent scholarship and the study of Jewish inscriptions have shown beyond doubt that the Jewish diaspora in the Roman empire continued to offer a vigorous religious life that was attractive to many Christians. In the later fourth century, while still a presbyter in Antioch, before he became bishop of Constantinople, John Chrysostom wrote a series of eight sermons designed to persuade Christians against what were obviously in fact common practices, frequenting synagogues and observing Jewish practices, and (contrary to the canons of the Council of Nicaea) calculating Easter according to the Jewish calendar. There were other reasons why Christians might defer to Jews; the very Scriptures were after all Hebrew texts, and few Christians knew Hebrew. Thus it was an important step when Jerome produced a new Latin translation of the Bible based on the Hebrew original, and encouraged his protégées to learn the language for themselves. But the rhetoric of John Chrysostom and many others after him who produced Christian polemics against Judaism was not benign. Even if it arose from a real situation which from their point of view needed to be addressed, the hostile and at times cruel rhetoric of these texts was to have long and regrettable results in the history of the church.

Even if this was in some senses a golden age of patristic writing, there was no 'triumph of Christianity' in the fourth century. Or if there was, it was bought at the cost of authoritarianism and even persecution. In the late fourth century the Emperor Theodosius I brought in a series of laws which set a momentous precedent. All sacrifices in pagan temples were henceforth strictly forbidden. It was this law which gave the signal for the destruction of the Serapaeum at Alexandria. Next Theodosius effectively outlawed paganism, forbidding not only sacrifice but all forms of pagan cult. A little later pagan priests had their privileges withdrawn; soon, pagan temples were the subjects of confiscation and pagans excluded from office.

In a fateful move, the arm of the state was also wielded against heretics. Not only wrong religion, but wrong Christian belief was to be the pretext for persecution. Augustine came to believe that this was right; he said so in the *City of God*, and the great Council of Carthage of 411, at which his was a central voice, licensed official action against the Donatists in North Africa by the Roman state. Heretics, particularly Arians, had already been the object of imperial laws in the 380s. In his youth Augustine had been a follower of Mani, founder of a rigorous dualist sect based on strict elitist principles, and Manichaeans too fell under imperial condemnation and became among the main victims of the persecuting state; they were deprived of legal rights, and informers against them were encouraged to come forward without fear of prosecution. However, the implementation of these laws was a different matter. While still a presbyter in Hippo, Augustine called a high-profile Manichaean to a public debate. Both tried to lay down their own terms, but Augustine emerged triumphant and reduced his opponent to silence: that was apparently enough. Augustine returned to the issue in a polemical work he wrote against Faustus, another North African Manichaean who had in fact been expelled from the province. A further debate between Augustine and a Manichaean, this time in person, took place in 404, and again Augustine prevailed; but Felix did not burn either; it was enough that he abjured Mani and all his teachings. Priscillian of Avila in Spain was an exceptional case of a so-called heretic, tarred with the brush of Manichaeanism, who was first exiled, then restored, and finally tried and executed at Trier on a charge of sorcery. Technically even he was not put to death for heresy. Yet even if not leading to an Inquisition, the existence of these laws must surely deprive late fourth-century Christianity of any credit for triumphal success.

It was if anyone Justinian, emperor in the sixth century, who laid claim to the role of Christian legislator and was seen as such by later Catholic historians. He codified Roman law and passed it on in the form of the Justinianic Code to the medieval west. He appears in this guise in the great frescoes of Raphael in the Stanza della Segnatura in the Vatican. Yet he also found it necessary to prosecute pagans, banning books and even putting some prominent men to death. He was still preoccupied with church unity, but his great Council of 553, its conclusions driven through only by breaking down the resistance of the bishop of Rome, in fact increased rather than settled the divide between east and west. The task of a Christian emperor in late antiquity was still not an easy one. The issuing of laws did not solve the matter, and the same problems carried on and on in new guises.

In the fifth century the Councils of Ephesus and Chalcedon epitomized many of the themes which I have identified in the latter part of this chapter. There was violence and personal rivalry; Nestorius the bishop of Constantinople was described by the church historian Socrates as 'disgracefully illiterate' and unacquainted with the writings of the ancients,[8] but he was pushed hard by Cyril, the bishop of Alexandria, and in 431 Nestorius was condemned by Cyril's council as a 'new Judas' and deposed. The Council recognized the Virgin Mary as the

'God-bearer' (*Theotokos*). A second Council at Ephesus in 449, known as the 'Robber Council', reinstated the anti-Nestorian Eutyches, and insulted the papal legates who were present. Two years later the Council of Chalcedon, held under a new emperor and attended by 520 bishops, reversed its judgment, condemned both Nestorius for separating the human and divine in Christ and Eutyches for his doctrine of a single nature, and reaffirmed the definitions of Nicaea in 325 and Constantinople in 381. The desire for a compromise was very great; there was much redrafting and lobbying behind the scenes, and the final draft was read out by the emperor himself. The emperor and empress were acclaimed as 'the torches of the orthodox faith', 'the new Constantine and Helena'. Nevertheless, much of the east regarded it as a fudge, and its rejection by many led to the separation of the Monophysites, who came to be identified with the Copts and the Jacobites or Syrian Orthodox. Justinian was still wrestling with this problem with his own council in 553.

Heresy was defined by the successful side in all these disputes, and heretics were called such only by the winning side. Epiphanius and many other writers of the period, including Eusebius of Caesarea, took the view that heresy was somehow like a disease, something 'out there', threatening the church like ravening wolves, or stirred up by the spirit of envy to disturb the peace of God. But the early church can no longer be seen in such monolithic terms, and conscious as we now are of the power of propaganda and the influence of the media to form opinion, we may now choose to see here a striking, and often regrettable, example of the mishandling of natural difference of opinion. This is not 'dissent' from an established norm, as in later centuries; at this point the very norm itself was still under formation, and the dissent and disagreement was part of the formation of orthodoxy. Frances Young has observed that it was a great mistake on the church's part to set off in the first place on the path of the verbal definition of faith, and certainly one can argue that councils caused as much trouble as they solved. One reading of the Council of Chalcedon is that it represented a mighty attempt to put a lid on all of this. If so it did not succeed. Some later emperors went so far as to pass imperial decrees forbidding further speculation, but that did not succeed either. Eastern emperors were still attempting to damp down theological argument in the eighth and ninth centuries, the heyday of dispute over Byzantine iconoclasm, and in the end this last great christological debate died out from sheer exhaustion.

In late antiquity the history of the church and the history of the Roman state became closely connected. Eusebius, and then Augustine after him, developed theories of the relationship of church and state which corresponded to their own historical experience a century apart. Few questioned the general right and duty of emperors to take up positions in church matters, except for the individual bishops like Athanasius who from time to time found themselves excluded by imperial decree. One may question how far this really affected the ordinary people of the empire, or the average monk or hermit, for whom the emperor was far away, but it did shape the hierarchical image of earth and heaven, and it presented the authority of God in the familiar terms of the authority of the emperor. Empire and church also shared the same problems, notably of preserving unity across such geographical and social divisions. On the other hand, late antiquity sees not only the spread of Christianity beyond the frontiers, to a Christian commonwealth of eastern kingdoms like Georgia, Armenia, and in Africa to Ethiopia and Nubia, but also, in contrast, the distinct signs of a widening gulf between west and east. At any rate before the age of Gregory the Great at the end of the sixth century, the bishop of Rome was not yet the pope of later centuries, but all the great councils of the period were principally eastern councils, at which the west was poorly represented at best. There was division between Constantinople and Rome in the fifth and sixth centuries, and Justinian's council did not help matters. But it was the political divide which followed the end of the Roman empire in the west and the establishment of the new barbarian kingdoms which drove a fateful wedge between east and west. Ironically, when these kingdoms in turn adopted Christianity, it was (as much by accident as from design) in several instances Arian Christianity which they embraced.

In the longer term, the foundation or renaming of Constantinople by Constantine the Great crystallized this incipient division and made possible a specifically Christian empire in the east. That outcome was not at all obvious even at the end of the fourth century, for the development of Christianity in Constantinople was a slow process. By the reign of Justinian in the sixth century we can genuinely describe it as a Christian city, and its population had reached its early peak when it approached half a million. Justinian set his sights on the recovery and restoration of the western empire, but it was a grand aim in which he was eventually to fail. There were still many ties, social, economic and religious, between the two parts of the Mediterranean at the end of the sixth century and on the eve of the Arab conquests. The eastern empire managed (just) to survive those shocks and to hold on to its conception of an orthodoxy shared by emperor and church. But the political fragmentation of the west, which Justinian was unable to halt, freed early medieval Christianity to take very different forms and different directions.

3

THE EARLY MIDDLE AGES

Henry Mayr-Harting

When did the Early Middle Ages begin? When did they end? Is this just the usual euphemism for the Dark Ages? Were the Dark Ages dark in point of evidence or in point of humanity? Or both? Will this lecture be at best the lecturer whistling to keep his courage in a dark tunnel, peering for light at the end of it? These must be the questions, if not on the lips of the polite, at least in their minds. Let me start with the beginning and end. Many would say that the beginning lay in monasticism and ascetic movements, which seemed to reverse the civic values of antiquity, and in the west they might point to the island monastery of Lérins and the composition around 550 of the Rule of St Benedict. These answers would be very valid. But as I have decided to be particularly concerned with how Christianity interacted with the secular world, which was above all the world of the newly settled Germanic peoples in the early medieval west, I should like to offer another answer. Nobody could doubt that clericalism, that is the idea of a clergy as a profession set apart, and the dynamic force in the salvation of society, became established during the Early Middle Ages. In 598 Pope Gregory the Great wrote a letter which shows that the Early Middle Ages had begun in the west, because it reveals the clericalist assumptions already as subconscious habits of mind. Someone had criticized the church of Rome for apeing the customs of Constantinople, for example introducing the *Kyrie eleison* at mass. This charge stuck in Gregory's gullet, and in admitting to the fact of the new custom, he defended himself as follows: 'We have neither said, nor do we say, *Kyrie eleison* as it is said by the Greeks. For among them, all the people sing it together; but with us it is sung by the clergy, and the people answer.'[1] There we already have medieval clericalism in a nutshell!

As regards the end of my period, I would single out, rather reluctantly considering the many possible criteria, the pontificate of a great pope, Gregory VII (1073–85). Gregory effected, with demonic personal drive, what has rightly been called a revolution, namely the centralization of jurisdiction and the day-to-day government of the church on Rome and the papacy. As is often the case with developments in the church at which many look askance, they are the more readily achieved by persons of deep religious and pastoral sense; and John Cowdrey, in his fine book on Gregory VII, has shown him to fit that description all right. It would be a great mistake to look back through Gregory VII-tinted spectacles at the Early Middle Ages. Everyone at that time, including the so-called Celtic church, accepted the papal primacy; but the primacy was a very different animal without the jurisdictional teeth which Gregory VII gave it.

To focus on the interaction of Christianity and the secular world of the Germanic peoples means, in the earliest centuries of the Early Middle Ages, watching how Christianity, while remaining in continuity with its doctrines and liturgy, allowed itself to be moulded in large degree to the mind-sets and social mores of the Germanic aristocracies. There is a brilliant study of this over twenty years ago by Patrick Wormald.[2] In a certain way, the nature of the Christian book, with its two testaments, facilitated this adaptation. The Old Testament featured familiar elements of the Germanic aristocratic mores: veneration of ancestors, war-hordes, and apparently justifiable feuds; only pagan cultic practices were firmly beyond the pale. Even there we perhaps consistently underrate the strength of religious syncretism in the early half of our period, on the part of those willing to accept the Christian God, but unwilling to take the risk of leaving their old pagan gods totally unpropi-tiated. If I were writing another lecture, I would be tempted to write it in terms of the church attempting, over the eighth to the eleventh centuries, to nudge people gently on from the Old to the New Testament. What I am interested in about the later Early Middle Ages, however, is the way a new Christian ethic began to pervade the Germanic political world. Here my paradigm is Charlemagne.

Charlemagne was king of the Franks from 768 to 814, and was crowned Roman Emperor in 800 by Pope Leo III in Rome. He was thus the originator of what, three and a half centuries later, would come to be called the Holy Roman Empire. Germanic barbarian kings had been Christians for a long time before him; but with them, their Christianity was a fact whereas with Charlemagne, who learned as his long reign progressed, it came to be a trust. I have been in trouble with Merovingianists for saying of the government finance of King Clovis the Frank around 500, that it consisted of swinging his battle axe into people's skulls and impounding their treasure. But there is little evidence that Christianity made much difference to the concept of rule of such characters before the eighth century. Whereas Charlemagne gathered to his court clerical and lay scholars from all over the west, collected many of the most important Christian writings in his library at Aachen, works necessary for what one might call applied Christianity, and established the professional study of Latin without which (in the west) there could be no grasp of the Christian Bible and culture.

There is a remarkable paradox about Charlemagne. Although his victories and conquests were incredible, including the Aquitanians and Catalans, the Saxons, the Lombards in Italy, and the Avars on the Middle Danube, he became most famous for a defeat, that at the pass of Roncesvalles in the Pyrenees when he was ambushed by Basques. This defeat came to be celebrated, yes celebrated, with full chivalric panoply, in the *Song of Roland* (*c.*1100). And then we come to a yet greater paradox about Charlemagne. Under this colossus there came in the idea, with full ruler encouragement, that kings and emperors should behave with humility. This imposing if portly figure, with his gargantuan appetite—and it seems not only for food—had a tailor-made, detailed, confession of sins composed for him by his leading court scholar, the York man, Alcuin.

It is true that Charlemagne had an almost vested interest in showing humility, for instance in not allowing his own image to be represented in any of the magnificent series of court manuscripts produced under his patronage. The *Libri Carolini*, largely composed by another of Charlemagne's court scholars, Bishop Theodulf of Orleans, maintained that the reason why the Byzantine emperors had lost their entitlement to be called Roman emperors, and would have to give way to Charlemagne, was that they had allowed images of themselves to be venerated. Babylonic pride had come before their fall! Hence, whether for fear of a cultic impropriety that would anger God, or out of a wish to show a moral claim to emperorship, it seemed prudent not to risk allowing his image to be venerated. But I am at present not so interested in Charlemagne's motives, as in the fact, the ways, and the consequences of humility becoming established as a royal virtue.

Near the end of Charlemagne's reign, an abbot of St Michael, Verdun, called Smaragdus, wrote a treatise, seemingly for Charlemagne, on how to be a king, a *Via Regia*. It dealt with the virtues proper to a king, each virtue being illustrated with a chain of examples mainly from Old Testament kings. This is the kind of thing meant by Old Testament kingship in our period. And it was the first time, so far as I know, that humility was explicitly treated in a theoretical work as an attribute of kingship. A king, said Smaragdus, should not glory in riches but in humility. Because David humbly confessed his wrong-doings (and David was Charlemagne's nickname in his own court), he was robed in splendour as priest and king. In order to humble Saul, continued our author, God said to him that it was when he was a child in his own eyes that he was made head of the tribes of Israel and was anointed king.[3] If we jump forward a century and a half, the biographer of Matilda, mother of the Emperor Otto I, held that her very prestige as a queen was a function of her personal humility. And in the Gospel Book of the Emperor Otto III, made about 996, and today at Aachen, is a splendid representation of the young emperor seated in majesty, and opposite this page a monk is depicted offering him the book, with the legend, 'O Emperor Otto, may God clothe your heart with this book (i.e. the Gospels)'.[4] Humility now *through* pictorial image!

If you ask me how much effect all this had on the actual behaviour of rulers, I have to admit that the Holy Spirit has not whispered into my ear how humble of heart it made them. But at some level they had reason to take it to heart. When rulers acknowledged their lowliness before God, paradoxically they gave a new loftiness to their ideal of God-given rule. We are here at a point where Christianity offered to rulers an enlarged concept of themselves; where, by offering them the option of humility, it actually enhanced their self-confidence! It also offered them, by presenting humility as a royal virtue, opportunities to make U-turns, which they needed or wanted to make, without too much loss of face. In 1003, for instance, the Emperor Henry II imprisoned Count Henry of Schweinfurt for a rebellion; but he really needed to free him because he depended on his support in the Upper Main region. Then in 1004 at Prague, while he was campaigning in Bohemia, he heard a sermon of Bishop Godescalc of Freising, which moved him to tears, on the parable of the servant forgiven a large debt by his master who then refused to forgive a small debt by a fellow servant to himself. Seen responding to this sermon in all humility, he at once released Count Henry.

It is quite clear what humility meant—listening to the church, as Old Testament kings had been required to listen to prophets or take the consequences. That might seem like a heavy price for accepting humility as a kingly virtue. But we must not read back into the Early Middle Ages the ideological conflicts between secular and ecclesiastical powers brought about by the revolution of Pope Gregory VII, never himself one to withhold a sword. One conclusion, however, seems inescapable from the idea of royal humility itself. Early medieval Christianity played a significant role in developing a vital notion in European history—that political power and authority should be limited. This depended on no sanctions other than those of God. It depended on the rulers' virtue and sense of moral responsibility; that and the constant yardstick which could be held up against their actions.

And who held up the moral yardstick to the churchmen, to whom kings were supposed to listen? This question would deserve a complex answer and I can here only give two simple ones. But again the answers depend upon conscience. First, Pope Gregory the Great, writing his *Pastoral Care* in the 590s, a runaway best-seller in the Middle Ages, stressed that the care of souls, indeed all rule, was a stewardship from God, a powerful and constantly repeated idea in the Middle Ages. Whatever his external authority, said Gregory, the pastor must judge himself inwardly, must turn the eye of his soul on his own infirmities, must make the law of the Lord his 'meditation all the day'.[5] Second, and earlier still but in a similar vein, Pope Leo I had spoken of the burden of priests, the *pondus sacerdotum*. This became a phrase to conjure with in the Early Middle Ages. The burden was that priests would have to answer for the souls of rulers at the day of judgement.

It could well be that the Englishman, the Venerable Bede, helped to float the idea of kingly humility onto the Carolingian world. His *Ecclesiastical History of the English People* (731) was widely read on the Continent at that time; there was a copy in Charlemagne's court library; and it had some unforgettable images of kings being what Bede called humble, i.e. listening to bishops. There was, for instance, Oswald translating the Irish words of the missionary Aidan into English for the benefit of his aristocracy, a sort of boast really that Oswald had passed his language tests; and there was Oswini prostrating himself at Aidan's feet to beg his pardon after a dispute about a horse, prompting Aidan to observe that Oswini would not last long, because he had never before seen a humble king.[6]

I would like to continue a little more with Charlemagne's religion and ethic, because it is revealing of how Christianity developed in the Early Middle Ages, not perhaps universally, but characteristically. Charlemagne gave a new and biblical dimension to what was meant by living under the law. What I have been describing so far is a Carolingian political morality which had nothing of constitutionalism to it, no Montesquieu-like checks and balances, but was brought about by a kind of interaction of moral awarenesses.

Perhaps it may have sounded, on the contrary, as if it was nothing of the sort but merely a construct imposed on Charlemagne by his clerical courtiers. Among many reasons why I utterly repudiate this, in favour of a genuine meeting of minds, is that Charlemagne was an inveterate conversationalist, who regarded his courtiers as friends, even being willing to accept a surprising degree of criticism from them. He particularly enjoyed the company of all and sundry while bathing, evidently in the nude, in the thermal springs of Aachen.[7] Charlemagne's experts were good at discovering fine springs, and then building palaces there. The bubbling springs at Paderborn are impressive to this day; but they were cold. The development of early medieval Christianity may owe more than meets the eye to the fact that those at Aachen were warm!

Now in Charlemagne's religion we have to balance aright the magical and ethical elements. There is no doubt that it had a highly propitiatory streak. The letter of 791 to Queen Fastrada, written when he was fighting the Avars, reveals it well. There were three days of litanies, says the king, to pray for safety and victory and to stave off the anger of God. There was abstinence from wine and meat, or a tariff of monetary compositions for those unwilling to observe it. Clerics who knew the psalms (by heart) were each to sing fifty, and all clerics were to walk barefoot while performing the litanies.[8] All this is scarcely surprising, considering the letter of less than seventy years earlier (723), in which Bishop Daniel of Winchester advised the great English missionary, St Boniface, how to argue with Germanic pagans in Hesse. Boniface is to put to them, not irritatingly but suavely, that they have no idea which of their gods is the most powerful god to propitiate, or what kind of sacrifices will most placate any of their gods.[9] This letter shows that deeply embedded in Germanic pagan religion was the appeasing of gods with correct cults and correct propitiatory sacrifices. But I would call the ethical side even stronger than this. Charlemagne attached importance to private and extra-liturgical prayer; an example is the Synod of Frankfurt (794). In presiding over this particular synod at an important royal palace of the Franks (as its name indicates), he was doing something very Constantine-like, certainly in conscious imitation of that emperor when he had presided over the Synod of Nicaea. As at Nicaea the lay ruler was presiding over a church gathering; and as at Nicaea an attempt was made to heal the divisions of Christians by condemning heresies, there Arianism, here adoptionism and iconodulism. Much of the legislation at Frankfurt, if legislation is the right word, was the repetition of legislation passed at early church councils. Frankfurt is a fascinating evocation of early Christian imperial times by one who would shortly be crowned Roman emperor. Clause 52, however, seems to be something entirely new in such a context. It says, 'let nobody believe that God can only be prayed to in the three languages (i.e. Hebrew, Greek and Latin) because God can be adored and man listened to in every language'—and here the vital proviso—'if he asks just things (*si iusta petierit*)'.[10] If this is magic, it is expressive magic rather than superstitious or compulsive magic, prayer expressive of the moral values of a society, prayer with regard to its inner meaning and right intention.

Most interesting of all is Charlemagne's concept of law, a fascinating mixture of symbolic magic in form and new ethical departures in content. When an early medieval ruler issued a law-code he was first and foremost projecting an image of himself and his rule in this very act, as Patrick Wormald has made abundantly clear. When Rothari, the Christian Lombard king in Italy, for example, produced his *Edict* in 643, the content had largely to do with customary Lombardic compensations for personal injuries and mutilations—what is paid if someone knocks out one of your front teeth, one of those which appear when smiling (16 shillings), as if anyone can be imagined to have risked smiling in such a society, or one of your molar teeth (8 shillings)—that kind of thing.[11] But for a Lombard king to produce a written code at all, whatever its content, reflected something of a Roman image. We have to wait until the time of Gregory VII before the primary purpose of issuing a collection of laws is to produce a judicially usable code, revealing a rational ordering of society, with legal procedures, principles, and precedents, and in the case of Anselm of Lucca's *Collectio Canonum*, with the papacy at the apex of that ordering. Anyone will understand why this should happen first in the late eleventh century who reads the admirably expounded story of Alexander Murray's *Reason and Society in the Middle Ages*.

So what image of his rule did Charlemagne project in his *Admonitio Generalis*, one of his great programmatic edicts, issued in 789 with Alcuin as his primary consultant?[12] First, a Constantinian one. Its first sixty out of eighty-two clauses were overwhelmingly directed to bishops and priests as the dynamic force in the salvation of society, and were based on the early councils beginning with that presided over by Constantine at Nicaea. It was Charlemagne's role, not to challenge the *sacerdotium*, but to make sure it did its job effectively. Second, it was an image of Old Testament kingship; the preamble compares Charlemagne to Josiah in his duty of admonition and correction. That is particularly interesting because a few decades later Carolingian churchmen were discussing Josiah as one who had failed despite being in the right, with the implication that conscience was a better indicator of God's will than was earthly success, as the superficial Orosius had taught in the fifth century. Third, it was an image of Moses as law-giver, for in the last twenty-two clauses, addressed to all people not just to the clergy, there is heavy use of the books of Leviticus and Deuteronomy as authorities. Constantine, David and Josiah, Moses—there you have the composite of how Charlemagne saw himself as ruler, law-giver, and war-leader. Not yet Christ. But the image of the ruler as Vicar of Christ would long since be in place to confront Gregory VII when he challenged the empire.

Now Leviticus and Deuteronomy contrast strongly with each other in character. There is some good sense in Leviticus, and some superstition in Deuteronomy; but broadly, if one wanted to make the magic/superstitious case about the ancient Israelites one would go to Leviticus, if the ethical case, one's book would be Deuteronomy. There is a hypothesis, which I have heard put forward with force by Oliver O'Donovan, that Josiah, who played no small part in human history by advancing the concept of living under law, used Deuteronomy as his basic law book. While Charlemagne could scarcely have had any idea of linking Deuteronomy and Josiah, he could well have had a sense of each half of this equation separately.

If we look at the direct citations in the *Admonitio* from Leviticus and Deuteronomy something extremely interesting emerges. There are five from Leviticus and four from Deuteronomy. But every one of the citations of Leviticus is taken from chapter 19, the one chapter where the book comes up for air and concerns itself with the love of God and neighbour. But the citations of Deuteronomy come from all over the book—from chapters 6, 16, 18, and 23—and concern a variety of subjects of prime importance to the Carolingians: love of God and neighbour again; just judgement and judges not receiving bribes; against divinations, for an important reason, 'because thou art instructed by the Lord God'; and keeping vows. In other words the authors of the *Admonitio*, as regards subject matter, were, much more than with Leviticus, thinking *through* Deuteronomy as a whole, and its moral implications for their own world.

At this stage I feel that I should acknowledge those enormous areas of my period which I am forced to neglect—monasticism and the ascendancy gained by the Rule of St Benedict in the west; missionaries, and the obstacles to converting peoples; developments in theological doctrines, particularly of the Eucharist the main lines of the debate about which, for many centuries to come, were laid out by two monks of Corbie in the ninth century; and most of all the development of parish religion. The extent to which village churches were established, with priests to minister in them, perhaps under the organization of the greater and richer monasteries, is something I should have wished to discuss, not least as a contribution of monasticism to grass-roots Christianity. Even more, within this context, would I have wanted to discuss the saints, their shrines and relics, and the constructive role of these in the establishment of Christianity as a social force. When recently I was at a conference in Paderborn connected to a magnificent exhibition about

Charlemagne to commemorate his meeting with Pope Leo III there in 799, immediately prior to his imperial coronation in Rome, I asked Stuart Airlie what he would talk about for this lecture if he were in my shoes. He at once replied, 'about the agonies of the saints', that is the social and personal agonies revealed by often ordinary people who resorted to their shrines. I would have followed this marvellous advice had it not been squeezed out by what I most wanted to say at present. Sherlock Holmes sometimes alludes to his unpublished cases—the case of the Two Coptic Patriarchs, or the murder which he spotted by the depth to which the parsley had sunk into the butter on a hot day—so that we are left wondering whether such cases would not be more interesting than what is published. Beware of the delusion!

Instead, I now turn from political morality to the subject of bishops. When Colin Morris wrote his masterpiece on the western church from 1050 to 1250, he aptly entitled it *The Papal Monarchy*. Such a title would make no sense for the preceding period. *Our* story is one of bishops. The prestige of the popes themselves came to them in no small measure from the conduct of their office as bishops of Rome. Henry Chadwick's inaugural lecture of 1959, *The Circle and the Ellipse*, posited two different structural models of the early church, one as if a circle with its centre at Jerusalem, the other linking the several churches by a line without one centre—an ellipse. We would have to say something like the latter about the church of the tenth and earlier centuries. In fact Rathier, bishop of Verona, did. He wrote in the 930s that the church was one in all its bishops; neither Jerusalem, nor Rome, nor Alexandria (he says, tucking Rome in the middle) had received a special prerogative of rule to the exclusion of others.[13] One in all its bishops: that is what at the time of the Second Vatican Council came frequently to be called collegiality. Pope Gregory the Great himself said almost exactly the same thing. When John, Patriarch of Constantinople, arrogantly started to adopt the style 'universal bishop', Gregory expostulated with him, saying that nobody should have this title. 'Are not all the bishops together clouds', he continued, 'who both rain in the words of preaching, and glitter in the light of good works?' Actually that was not quite all he said, because despite his fraternal mode, he never allowed papal primacy to be forgotten. He said that if anyone should be called universal bishop it should be himself, but in truth no one should be.[14]

An influential early medieval bishop was Caesarius, bishop of Arles 502–42. He had been a monk of Lérins and illustrated what a reputation for monastic asceticism and generosity to the poor could do for episcopal authority. Above all he was a great preacher, though like Gregory the Great, he regarded the most important form of preaching as the example of one's life. His sermons on everyday pastoral matters were delivered in simple language and a loud voice, though he still had to stop people talking during them! Eventually he collected them into an edition, so that, as his Preface says, they could be recited to the people by priests and deacons in his diocese.[15] He said that he had thereby secured for the parochial clergy the power of making the word (*verbum faciendi potestas*). Later these sermons extended Caesarius's influence far beyond his diocese, because they proved to be just what many Carolingian bishops needed for their office and authority.

At the other end of our period, Thietmar, bishop of

Merseburg, who began writing his wonderfully rich and interesting *Chronicle* about the Empire around 1018, expresses the episcopal mentality to perfection. He accepted the papal primacy, even saying that Otto I should not have criticized Pope Benedict V, who was his superior. But he has a remarkable passage, showing both how high he pitched episcopal majesty, and how implicitly he accepted that the proper subordination of bishops was to the lay ruler rather than the pope. By now the lay ruler, king or emperor, was Vicar of Christ. Declaring how right Otto I was to wrest the appointment of bishops in Bavaria from the hands of a mere Duke of Bavaria, Thietmar says:

For our kings and emperors, who take the place of the Almighty Ruler in this world, are set above all pastors, and it is entirely incongruous that those whom Christ has constituted princes of this earth (i.e. bishops), should be under the dominion of any but those who excel all mortals by the blessing of God and the glory of their crown.

Thietmar has numerous vignettes of bishops not least concerning their celebration of Mass, such as Archbishop Tagino of Magdeburg, who would be very stern before celebrating, but all smiles and cheerfulness afterwards.[16]

Given the conditions of the time in the empire, which were a lack of bureaucracy or local machinery of law and order, kingship being itinerant and politics patrimonial or face-to-face, no bishop could hold his own in the localities without being generally acceptable to the aristocracy of the region. This is a point that has been well brought out by Timothy Reuter. Take Worms as an example. We have an extraordinary account of the bishops appointed to this see in 999 to 1000, a topical year. Young bishop Franco died unexpectedly in Rome on 27 August 999, after spending a fortnight dressed in a hair shirt, fasting and praying, in a grotto next to the church of S. Clemente, together with his friend, the nineteen-year-old, deeply religious and highly-strung Emperor Otto III. A month later the emperor named his young friend and former chaplain whom he had made abbot of Farfa, Erpo of Halberstadt, as bishop. Three days later, before he could make a move, Erpo died suddenly and was laid to rest in Farfa. Next Otto appointed another of his young chaplains to be bishop, who was so keen that he set out from Rome with alacrity; but at Chur on the way, he also died.[17] What one would never guess from this story as told, was that all three men, and Burchard who became bishop in 1000 and lasted for twenty-five years, belonged to the same aristocratic clan of Hesse, which was powerful in the region of Worms. The fact that the ruler had in his chapel devout, ambitious chaplains, who travelled about with him, and who, being drawn from aristocratic families, would step acceptably into one bishopric or another in the course of time, is all striking testimony to the way the interests and religious purposes of rulers and aristocracy tended to coalesce rather than be in conflict with each other where the church was concerned.

One of the best examples I can give of a tenth-century Ottonian bishop, as a mixture—aristocrat to the core, deep involvement with the ruler, and high religious aims—is Hildiward of Halberstadt. He came from a great Frankish family on his father's side and almost certainly a Saxon one on his mother's. He was chaplain to bishop Bernhard of Halberstadt, who had been bishop for forty-five years when he died and

Hildiward succeeded him. Hildiward and Bernhard were designated as bishops by their predecessors, which was clean against canon law, but often happened, and was a mark of trust, and frequently also of blood relationship. Hildiward was bishop for twenty-nine years, from 968 to the end of 996. My own time as Fellow and Medieval History Tutor at St Peter's was almost exactly the same years, a millennium on—1968–1997. Hildiward set about rebuilding his cathedral. It was consecrated on 21 October 991, in the presence of the 11-year-old Otto III, his Burgundian grandmother, and many archbishops and bishops. It was precisely attendance at such occasions by kings and emperors that built up their sacrality. October 21st was the feast of St Gall, to whom Hildiward had a special devotion, because he had himself been educated at the famous imperial monastery of St Gall, in modern Switzerland. In the consecration of the cathedral, the bishop's faithful chaplain Hildo (who must also have been a relative) helped him in everything and made very prudent arrangements. Thietmar adds—and one must remember that at this time the statements of ceremony and ritual were generally more powerful than those of theoretical writers: 'never before or after, so truthful men affirm, was everything in divine praises and secular affairs done so fully and so acceptably to everyone.'

When Hildiward lay on his death bed he called his chaplain Wulfhar to him. 'Do you see anything, brother?' the bishop asked. Wulfhar replied that he saw nothing. Whereupon Hildiward told him that the room in which he lay was that in which his two predecessors had died and—here a whopping piece of episcopal exaltation—was 'full of divine majesty'.[18]

Yet Thietmar, recording the assent of Otto I to Hildiward's becoming bishop of Halberstadt in 968, wrote something, in a most matter of fact way, which made my hair stand on end when I first read it several decades ago. Hildiward's father, Eric, had been the ringleader of a plot to assassinate Otto I at his Easter court of 941 in Quedlinburg, for which Otto ordered him to be beheaded. Now in 968, as the Emperor handed Hildiward the pastoral staff, he said, 'with this, receive the price of your father'.[19] All those years both men had been aware of the state of blood-feud between them because of Eric's death; and now at last the emperor was making material compensation, or paying a wergild (man-price), accepted as such by the very Hildiward who died surrounded by divine majesty, with the bishopric of Halberstadt. I think it safe to say that Gregory VII would not have liked this, and that less than two centuries later anything like it would have been totally impossible. But in the tenth century, such was the intertwining of the sacralities of church and rule, such the solvent of political tensions.

The great bishops of the Early Middle Ages were Holy Men, noblemen Holy Men, *Adelsheiliger*, as the Germans have called them. Caesarius of Arles, Wilfrid of York, Hincmar of Rheims, Bruno of Cologne, and Hildiward of Halberstadt, to name but a few, were all *Adelsheiliger*. Holiness, however, is not an absolute concept, but one to some extent relative to the societies in which it is found. So what do I mean by holiness in bishops? Effective early medieval bishops were pillars of rule and order in their dioceses. That could not mean that constitutional powers were delegated to them, which would be a nonsensical concept in an age when rule was not so much constitutionalist as face-to-face. The powers of bishops were exercised much more informally. At one level, in that magic-penetrated society, holiness was the capacity to handle supernatural power so that it ostensibly sparked to life on this earth. A bishop lit up supernatural power by expensive and seemingly miraculous building works, by the sounds of music with which he could fill those buildings (which accounts for Ethelwold of Winchester's craze for building organs wherever he went), by the saints' relics and other treasures he could acquire, by his personal presence and the terror it could inspire amongst the powerful, as well as the love among the poor.

It has to be admitted that the awe which such bishops inspired was heightened by the little armies which they raised from their estates and often led personally into the field. These were the struts of holiness. Bishop Michael of Regensburg, for instance, went off to fight the Hungarians in the 940s. He returned from a (losing) battle against them, minus an ear, but with greatly enhanced kudos.[20]

Not all early medieval bishops by a long chalk were holy, of course, on any showing of that word, but, to speak only of the century and a half before the Gregorian Reform, an extraordinary number were considered to be so. When Sir Richard Southern discussed Gregory VII's at first sight outlandish claim that a duly ordained pope was undoubtedly made a saint by the merits of St Peter, he pointed to the fact that some hundred of Gregory's 150 or so predecessors as pope were actually venerated as saints. One could say something similar about bishops in the imperial system which Gregory challenged, where bishops and ruler were so part and parcel of each other. What Gregory had on his hands was not a corrupt system which could easily be brushed off, but a remarkably holy one. That was the real challenge to papal leadership, when the papacy came to challenge the imperial episcopal system.

Looking back over my lecture at the end, I must add a third ingredient to those elements in early medieval religion which I have called magic and morality. That third ingredient is spirituality, which I touched on in speaking of Charlemagne and prayer. We can be *too* relativist about the Christian religion down the ages. The overt manipulations of the supernatural which I have mentioned, would have meant nothing at the time, had they not been perceived as grounded in a life of prayer and devotion, such as we understand perfectly well today. Many prayer-books and collections of private prayers survive from the tenth century, one at least belonging to a magnificent bishop, Archbishop Egbert of Trier, and there is much evidence that bishops tried to say the psalms in private if they were unable to attend the public offices. There is a little prayer-book of private prayers in Latin, which belonged to the Emperor Otto III himself. I was able to spend a glorious Saturday morning in May 1976 studying it, when it was still in the Library of Schloss Pommersfelden near Bamberg. When I read in one of the prayers, addressed to Jesus, 'be mild to me as you were to Mary the whore, and fill my eyes with tears as you filled hers, when she washed your feet and wiped them with her hair', I did not feel that one needed to be a tenth-century Christian in order to understand.[21]

4

EASTERN CHRISTIANITY

Kallistos Ware

Around the year 1750 two men were talking in a tavern
opposite one of the theatres in central London. 'I bet you',
said the first, 'that, if I undertake to perform something that
is manifestly impossible, and invite the public to come and
see me do it, there will be so many fools willing to accept the
invitation that they will fill the theatre opposite.' His companion agreed to the wager. The two friends hired the theatre
and distributed handbills, announcing that on a specified
evening a gentleman of quality would ascend the stage and
place himself inside a beer bottle. While in the bottle he would
sing the National Anthem, along with other patriotic songs;
and members of the audience would be welcome to come on
to the stage and inspect the bottle while he was singing inside
it. Some days before the appointed evening, every seat in the
theatre had been sold. Meanwhile the two friends prudently
left London for a week in the country. The audience arrived to
find the stage of the theatre entirely empty except for a table

with a beer bottle placed upon it; but no gentleman of quality ascended the stage and offered to get inside the bottle. After a time the audience grew bored and broke up the furnishings of the theatre, creating a vast bonfire in the street outside. But at any rate the first of the two friends had won his bet.[1]

Tonight I feel precisely in the situation of someone who has offered to get inside a beer bottle and sing the National Anthem. For it is my task to recount, within the narrow limits of a fifty-minute lecture, the many-sided story of Eastern Christianity from the fifth to the fifteenth century. I have promised to do something that is manifestly impossible, and yet you have all come to witness me do it. Unwisely I have not left for a week in the country, and so I must do what I can to meet your expectations.

Let me arrange my remarks under three headings, of which the first will occupy the greater part of my time: division, development, and deification.

- First, *division*: my story will be one of increasing fragmentation, initially within the confines of the Christian east, and then between the Greek east and the Latin west.
- Second, *development*: while gradually cut off from its Christian neighbours on the eastern and subsequently on the western side, by way of counterbalance the Byzantine church embarked upon a vast missionary advance northwards into the Slav lands.
- Third, *deification* (in Greek *theosis*): we shall be looking at the master theme that characterizes eastern Christian theology, more especially from the eighth century onwards, and this is

a deepening concern with the manner in which holiness is transmitted to each believer.

I: DIVISION

What above all makes my task little less than an impossibility is the fact that, while Eastern Christianity may from one point of view be regarded as a unity, a distinct and coherent whole, it is at the same time a highly complex unity. Let us take a quick overview of the situation around the year 400.

Within the East Roman or Byzantine empire there was a predominantly Greek-speaking church, with its chief centre at the imperial capital Constantinople. But alongside Constantinople there were other major centres within the East Roman empire: Alexandria, with jurisdiction over Egypt (here the great majority of Christians spoke not Greek but Coptic); Antioch, with jurisdiction over Syria (here a large proportion of the faithful were Syriac-speaking); and Jerusalem, which unlike the places so far mentioned was not important administratively or commercially, but which has always enjoyed a special position within the Christian world as the place where Christ suffered on the cross and rose from the dead. Then, outside the frontiers of the Roman empire, there were Christian churches in Persia, Georgia, Armenia, Ethiopia, and India.

At the outset of the fifth century the Christians in all these areas were basically in communion with each other. But there was no single administrative centre on which they all depended, and no single hierarch endowed with direct authority over them all. There was merely a loosely structured federation of local churches. Moreover, these local churches possessed varying theological approaches, employed different forms of worship, and used a multiplicity of languages: Greek, Coptic, Syriac, Georgian, Armenian, and (in Ethiopia) Ge'ez. While there was an overall unity of faith and sacramental fellowship, there was certainly no uniformity.

From the fifth century onwards, however, there ensued a progressive fragmentation, occurring in two stages: first, during the fifth to the seventh century the Christian east became split into three groups; then, during the ninth to the thirteenth century there developed an increasing estrangement between the Greek east, with its centre at Constantinople, and the Latin west, with its centre at Rome. How and why did this disintegration come about?

(i) *The Church of the East*

So far as the first stage is concerned—the fragmentation within eastern Christianity—this came about in two sub-stages, the first of which led to the separate existence of the Church of the East, the second to the creation of a family of 'Oriental' or 'non-Chalcedonian' churches. The first of these sub-stages was a consequence of the Council of Ephesus (431); the second, of the Council of Chalcedon (451).

For Byzantine Orthodoxy, as for Roman Catholicism and Anglicanism, the 431 Council of Ephesus constitutes the third Ecumenical Council. But its main decision—the declaration that the Blessed Virgin Mary is 'God-Birthgiver' (*Theotokos*) or 'Mother of God'—was not acceptable to many Christians belonging to the theological tradition of Antioch. They took as their guide Theodore of Mopsuestia (*c.*350–428), perhaps the greatest of the Patristic commentators on the Bible, often styled 'The Interpreter'. Theodore placed strong emphasis upon the distinct existence, within the one incarnate Christ, of two complete natures, the one divine and the other human. It was Theodore's aim to allow full scope for our Lord's human freedom, and so for the true reality of the human temptations that he underwent: 'tempted in everything just as we are, only without sinning' (Heb. 4: 15). For this reason, Theodore and others in the Antiochene tradition, although genuinely convinced that Christ is one, were reluctant to say that Mary is in the strict sense 'Mother of God', for fear that this would diminish the integrity of Christ's manhood. As they saw it, Mary is mother only of the human 'temple' in which God the Word came to dwell.

Theodore was dead by the time the Council of Ephesus met, but his viewpoint was upheld by Nestorius, Patriarch of Constantinople during 428–31. The chief advocate of the title *Theotokos*, and the unrelenting opponent of Nestorius, was St Cyril, Patriarch of Alexandria (d. 444). As Cyril insisted in the first of his Twelve Anathemas, 'If anyone does not acknowledge Emmanuel to be truly God, and hence the Holy Virgin to be Mother of God—for she gave fleshly birth to God the Word made flesh—let him be anathema.'[2] Mary, that is to say, is not the mother of a man more or less closely associated with God the Word, but she is mother of a single undivided person, God and Man at once, the divine Logos made flesh.

Those who—following the Christological approach of Theodore and the Antiochene 'school'—refused to accept the decisions of Ephesus, came eventually to form a separate communion, known as the Church of the East. This was Syriac-speaking and was situated almost entirely outside the East Roman empire, under the rule of the Persian Sassanids, its main centres being in Mesopotamia (approximately modern Iraq). Sometimes it is called the 'Assyrian' or 'Nestorian Church'. While the first title is acceptable, the second is definitely not. For the Church of the East holds Theodore of Mopsuestia in far higher esteem than Nestorius; and it certainly does not endorse the opinion commonly attributed to Nestorius, that the incarnate Christ consists of two distinct persons—in the modern sense of the word 'person'—coexisting in a single body. (Indeed, Nestorius himself never believed that.) There is in fact no good reason to accuse the Church of the East of heresy in its understanding of Christ; and significantly in 1994 its present head, Mar Dinkha IV, signed a highly positive Christological agreement with Pope John Paul II.

One aspect of Assyrian church history that is little known in the West is the astonishing dynamism of its missionary work. In this connection a Scots Presbyterian author, John Stewart, aptly speaks of 'a Church on fire'.[3] By the early seventh century missionaries from the Church of the East had travelled as far as India and north-west China. Marco Polo, on his journey to the Far East during 1271–5—if, that is to say, he ever actually went there—found Assyrian Christian communities in almost all the cities that he visited. This missionary expansion is the more impressive, when we reflect that the Church of the East was never a state church but was, on the contrary, subject at times to persecution. In their preaching of the Christian faith its members did not enjoy any political support, and so their advance across Asia was in no way an expression of 'colonialism'.

From the fourteenth century onwards the Church of the East was increasingly oppressed by the Mongols and suffered drastic losses, becoming largely restricted to the mountains of Kurdistan. One relatively bright episode, in what is otherwise a melancholy chronicle of decline, was the establishment of 'The Archbishop of Canterbury's Assyrian Mission', whose story—likewise little known in the West—has been recounted in fascinating detail by Dr J. F. Coakley.[4] Established by Archbishop Benson in 1885, this continued to function until 1915. A remarkable, if not unique, feature of the mission was that it had as its basic principle the firm resolve not to convert a single Assyrian Christian to Anglicanism, an ideal to which it remained faithful up to the end. How many other missions, in the past or today, have shown such generosity towards their fellow Christians? Sadly, during and after the First World War, the Assyrians were victims of genocide and 'ethnic cleansing' at the hands of the Turks and Kurds, and there are today only a few of them left in their homelands, while the majority now live in exile.

Outstanding among the writers in the Church of the East is St Isaac of Nineveh (seventh century), who—under the name 'Isaac the Syrian'—has long been widely read and greatly loved throughout the Greek and Slav worlds. Few if any of the Byzantine Christians who regarded Isaac as the quint-essence of Orthodoxy realized that he belonged to what was, in their eyes, the doctrinally suspect 'Nestorian' Church. Isaac was a theologian of divine love, who believed that in the end God's inexhaustible compassion will prove triumphant over human sin, so that all will eventually be saved. Along with Origen, St Gregory of Nyssa, and Julian of Norwich, he dared to hope that

> All shall be well, and
> All manner of thing shall be well.[5]

As Isaac the Syrian affirms of the ever-loving Creator:

> I am of the opinion that he is going to manifest some wonderful outcome, a matter of immense and ineffable compassion. . . . It is not [the way of] the compassionate Maker to create rational beings in order to deliver them over mercilessly to unending affliction. . . . God is not one who requites evil, but he sets aright evil.[6]

> Far be it, that vengeance could ever be found in that Fountain of love and Ocean brimming with goodness![7]

(ii) *The Non-Chalcedonians*

Turning now to the second sub-stage in the fragmentation of the Christian east, we find that a further division came to pass as a result of the Council of Chalcedon (451). This is reckoned as the fourth Ecumenical Council by Byzantine Orthodoxy and by the Christian west, but it proved unacceptable to a substantial number of eastern Christians, particularly in Egypt and Syria. In order to counteract the false teaching of Eutyches—who, so his critics alleged, claimed that the human aspect of Christ had been swallowed up in the divine—the Chalcedonian Fathers affirmed that the incarnate Saviour is one person (*hypostasis*) in two complete natures (*physeis*), the one divine and the other human. The opponents of Chalcedon believed that Christ the God-Man (*Theanthropos*) is indeed fully and genuinely human; and most of them, at any rate in the period after Chalcedon, dissociated themselves from Eutyches. They were willing to say that Christ is '*from* [or *out of*] two natures', but they believed that the Chalcedonian formula '*in* two natures' implied the kind of division between the divine and human aspects of Christ for which Nestorius had been condemned. This they saw as a betrayal of St Cyril of Alexandria who, although using the phrase 'from two natures', had also employed the slogan 'one incarnate nature (*physis*) of God the Word'. In fact Chalcedon appealed with great emphasis to the authority of Cyril, and it reaffirmed the title *Theotokos*; but this was not enough to satisfy many of Cyril's disciples.

Most Christians today might be inclined to regard the difference between the phrases 'from two natures' and 'in two natures' as minimal, so long as it is agreed that Christ at his incarnation took integral humanness. Obviously a great deal depends on the way in which we understand the term 'nature' (*physis*): does it signify 'set of distinctive characteristics, existing in a specific and concrete way' (in which case Christ has two natures), or does it correspond more closely to what we today mean by 'personality' or 'personal subject' (in which case Christ has or is one *physis*)? But in the two centuries following Chalcedon Christians were for the most part unwilling to regard the dispute as merely linguistic. Although strenuous efforts were made to secure a reconciliation, in the end these came to nothing.

Schemes for reunion between the Chalcedonians and the non-Chalcedonians were promoted in particular by different emperors. Constantine (d. 337), the first Christian emperor, was inspired by the ideal of one universal empire supported by one undivided church. This meant that, for him and his successors, disputes over doctrine were not simply an internal matter for the church but had political implications; schisms between Christians undermined the unity and stability of the empire. Yet, despite imperial pressure, the Chalcedonian controversy was not resolved.

In the tortuous doctrinal discussions between 451 and 681, two moments are particularly important: the fifth and the sixth Ecumenical Councils. The second Council of Constantinople (553)—for Byzantine Orthodoxy, the fifth Ecumenical Council—met under the presidency of the Emperor Justinian, rebuilder of the great Church of the Holy Wisdom (St Sophia), which still stands in the centre of modern Istanbul as a symbol of Byzantine Orthodoxy, although long since converted into a mosque. In an attempt to win over the non-Chalcedonians, the 553 Council reinterpreted Chalcedon from a Cyrilline perspective, insisting on the need to employ a plurality of formulae. It is essential, said the Council, to say both that Christ has one nature and that he has two; both that he is 'from two natures' and that he is 'in two natures'. The two sets of formulae counterbalance one another; to use the one set without the other is misleading. What matters, that is to say, is not terminology as such, but the manner in which the terms are understood; we must reach out beyond words to the realities which they denote.

The 553 Council also adopted 'theopaschite' language (language that attributes suffering to God), proclaiming in its tenth anathema, 'He who is crucified in the flesh, our Lord Jesus Christ, is true God and Lord of glory and one of the

Holy Trinity' (compare 1 Cor. 2: 8). In this way the 553 Council at Constantinople continued the work of the 431 Council at Ephesus. Just as Ephesus, in endorsing the title *Theotokos*, had affirmed 'God was born', so now the 553 Council stated 'God died'. But in both cases there was added the vital qualification 'in the flesh'. Christ did not undergo birth and death in his divine nature, for God *qua* God is not born and does not die. It is the second person of the Trinity, not the divine nature, that makes his own the experience of human birth and human death; and he does so, not in his eternal state as God, but by virtue of his incarnation.

If the 553 Council continued the work of Ephesus, then the third Council of Constantinople (680–81)—for Byzantine Christendom, the sixth Ecumenical Council—continued the work of Chalcedon. During the 620s and 630s a compromise had been proposed, which it was hoped would reconcile Chalcedonians and non-Chalcedonians: although Christ has two natures, it was argued, he has only a single energy (monoenergism) and a single will (monotheletism), because in practice the two natures always act in conjunction with one another. To this the 680–81 Council rejoined that human nature, without its own distinctive human energy and human will, would be an unreal abstraction. The humanity of Christ is not a puppet show worked from behind the scenes by the divine Logos, but the incarnate Saviour possesses genuine human freedom. In this way, without reinstating Theodore of Mopsuestia, the Council reaffirmed what had been his major concern. The incarnate Christ, so the Fathers of 680–81 concluded, has 'two natural wills and two natural energies'; the two wills are never opposed to each other, but the human will remains at all times voluntarily obedient to the divine.

When the third Council of Constantinople met, however, the question of reunion with the non-Chalcedonians had become largely theoretical. This was because the situation in the Eastern Mediterranean had been fundamentally altered by the sudden rise of Islam. When Mohammed died in 632, his authority was limited to a small area of the Arabian peninsula. But within fifteen years his followers had defeated the armies of Byzantium and had overrun Syria, Palestine, and Egypt; within fifty years the Arabs were at the walls of Constantinople and almost captured the city; within a hundred they had crossed from North Africa into Spain, and forced western Europe to fight for its life at the Battle of Poitiers (732). Christendom survived, but only just. The three patriarchates of Alexandria, Antioch, and Jerusalem were lost to the Byzantines. This meant that the areas in Egypt and Syria occupied by the non-Chalcedonians now lay outside the boundaries of the empire, and so from the political viewpoint there no longer existed an urgent need to promote ecclesiastical reconciliation.

Both the Chalcedonians and the non-Chalcedonians produced theologians of eminence. Of particular influence on the non-Chalcedonian side was Severus of Antioch (*c.*465–538), a subtle and perceptive thinker; he was not an extremist, but he was firm in his refusal to accept Chalcedon. Among the Chalcedonians the greatest writer was St Maximus the Confessor (*c.*550–662), a contemporary of St Isaac the Syrian, although it seems improbable that either knew anything of the

other. In his Christology Maximus insisted upon the significance of Christ's human will; it is precisely because we see in
Christ authentic human freedom, constantly co-operating
with the divine will, that he constitutes for us a model and
example that we humans may imitate. As a mystical theologian
Maximus took up, and stated in more balanced form, the ideas
of the mysterious author who wrote under the name of
Dionysius the Areopagite (*c.*500). More particularly, Maximus
believed, in common with Duns Scotus in the thirteenth-
century west, that God would have become incarnate even if
humankind had never lapsed into sin. The birth of the Saviour
at Bethlehem is not merely a contingency plan, devised by
God in response to the fall, but it is part of God's eternal
purpose from before the creation of the world. So Maximus
asserts concerning the incarnation: 'This is the great and
hidden mystery, this is the blessed end on account of which
all things were created. This is the divine purpose foreknown
prior to the beginning of created things.'[8] Yet this cosmic
Christ, who embraces and recapitulates the totality of the
created order and the whole of human history, also undergoes
a personal incarnation in the heart of each one of us. Like
Meister Eckhart, Maximus speaks of the birth of the Lord in
every human soul: 'The divine Word of God wills to effect the
mystery of his incarnation at all times and in everyone. . . . It is
always Christ's will to be born mystically, becoming incarnate
through those who are saved, and making the soul that gives
him birth a virgin mother.'[9]

The Christians who felt unable to accept the Council of
Chalcedon exist today as a family of six self-governing
churches:

(1) The Syrian Orthodox Church
(2) The Syrian Orthodox Church in India (an offshoot of (1), founded according to tradition by the Apostle Thomas)
(3) The Coptic Orthodox Church (in Egypt)
(4) The Ethiopian Orthodox Church
(5) The Eritrean Orthodox Church (independent of (4) since 1994)
(6) The Armenian Orthodox Church

Collectively these six churches are often styled 'The Oriental Orthodox Church', as distinct from the Byzantine (Chalcedonian) Church, which is called 'The Eastern Orthodox Church'. This is a useful terminological distinction, even though etymologically the words 'oriental' and 'eastern' are equivalent. In the past the Oriental or non-Chalcedonian Orthodox were commonly called 'Monophysites'. This is in itself justifiable, since—following St Cyril of Alexandria—they ascribe to Christ only one nature (although it might be more accurate to designate them 'Miaphysite' rather than 'Monophysite'). But the designation could be misleading, since in the west 'Monophysite' has usually been taken to signify 'Eutychian' (that is, 'denying to Christ full humanity'); and, as we have noted, this is not in fact the standpoint of the Oriental Orthodox. Since they themselves usually prefer not to use the term 'Monophysite', it is best avoided.

Since 1964 there has been a promising 'dialogue' between the Eastern and the Oriental Orthodox, at first on an unofficial and then on an official basis. In 1989 the two sides, at a conference in Amba Bishoy Monastery, Egypt, affirmed that they recognized each other as confessing in common 'the apostolic faith of the undivided church of the first centuries'. More specifically, they stated that the Christological difficulties of the past had been resolved; while using different terminology, both sides believe that Christ is truly God and truly human. They urged that on this basis, as a matter of urgent priority, there should now be a restoration of full sacramental communion between the two ecclesial families. Regrettably this has not yet happened.

As a result, then, of the schisms that occurred in the period between the fifth and the seventh centuries, the Christian east became divided into three bodies:

(1) The Church of the East (numbering today about 250,000–400,000).

(2) The six Oriental Orthodox Churches (numbering today about 30 million).

(3) The Byzantine or Eastern Orthodox Church. Through expansion northward, this has come to include the Romanians and most of the Slavs. It exists at present as a federation of fourteen (some would say, fifteen) self-governing or 'autocephalous' churches, numbering perhaps 120 million members.

(iii) *Constantinople and Rome*

It is time to move on to the second major stage in the fragmentation of the Christian world, the division between the Byzantine Orthodox Church in the Greek east, and the Roman Catholic Church in the Latin west. It will be helpful to start by asking: Should we think of this east–west schism as an *event* or a *process*? The 'popular', non-specialist view, at any rate in the past, saw the schism as an event, or more exactly as two connected events. There was first during 861–7 a preliminary conflict between Pope Nicolas I of Rome and Patriarch Photius of Constantinople—the 'Photian schism' or the 'Nicolite schism', depending on our point of view. At this point the two main factors in the schism—the *Filioque* and the papal claims—were brought clearly into the open, but matters were not as yet carried to their logical conclusion, and communion between Rome and Constantinople was quickly restored. Then in 1054 there came the exchange of mutual anathemas between the papal legate, Cardinal Humbert, and the patriarch of Constantinople, Michael Cerularius; and this marked the 'final consummation' of the schism.

Among specialists, however, it has long been recognized that such a view as this constitutes a gravely misleading oversimplification. Rather than treating the schism as a single or twofold event, we should regard it—in the words of a great Oxford Byzantinist, the Dominican Gervase Mathew—as 'a gradual, fluctuating, disjointed process, perhaps not consummated till the end of the fifteenth century, and perhaps only reaching its present shape about 150 years later'.[10] Specific incidents, such as the conflict between Photius and Nicolas in the 860s or the exchange of anathemas in 1054, can only be properly assessed if placed in the context of this far broader 'process'—a process whose origins extend back much earlier than the ninth or the eleventh century, and whose final completion, as Fr Gervase suggests, did not come about until the seventeenth or even the early eighteenth century.

This slowly evolving process may best be characterized as a

gradual *estrangement*, to borrow the term used by another great Dominican, Yves Congar.[11] Long before there was a final schism the Greek east and the Latin west had become strangers to one another; and it is precisely because of this mutual estrangement that specific incidents such as the 'Photian schism' or the confrontation between Humbert and Cerularius were potentially so dangerous. Exactly when the estrangement developed into a formal separation it is hard to say; certainly it did not happen simultaneously at a single moment throughout the eastern Mediterranean. The general and all-embracing schism between east and west grew out of a series of local schisms, many of them at first temporary in character.

In the process of estrangement, far more important than the exchange of anathemas in 1054—which was in any case quickly forgotten by both sides—was the sack of Constantinople in 1204 by members of the Fourth Crusade. Tragically this is something which, as Sir Steven Runciman remarks, 'could never be forgiven nor forgotten by the Christians of the East'.[12] Henceforward the Greeks saw the Latins, not as fellow Christians who differed from themselves on certain points of faith and ritual, but as ruthless enemies of their church and nation. It has to be remembered, however, that it was a faction of the Greeks that initially invited the Crusaders to enter Constantinople; had it not been for Byzantine intrigue, the disaster might never have happened. Even so, this does not in any way justify the three days of fearful pillage in which the Crusaders indulged.

Yet the year 1204 is far from marking the final consummation of the schism. Until the capture of Constantinople by the

Turks in 1453 there were continuing efforts at reunion, in particular at the second Council of Lyons (1274), and more seriously at the Council of Ferrara-Florence (1438–9). Despite the failure of these efforts, as late as the seventeenth century there were frequent examples of co-operation and even eucharistic intercommunion between the Greeks and the Latins, not only in Venetian dominions but also in places under Ottoman rule. The Jesuit Joseph Besson, in a book published in 1660, says of the work of the Roman Catholic missionaries in the Near East, 'The Greeks and the Syrians open their houses to the apostolic men; they open even their church doors and their pulpits. The parish priests welcome our assistance, the bishops beg us to cultivate their vineyards.'[13] Above all, in the patriarchate of Antioch the schism did not become a fixed and firm reality until 1724; indeed, in Syria and Lebanon there has never been a time when intercommunion between Catholics and Orthodox has altogether ceased.

Although the Council of Ferrara-Florence failed to establish an all-embracing union between Rome and the Christian east, it did lead—more particularly from the late sixteenth century onwards—to the establishment of various Eastern Catholic churches, especially in Ukraine, Slovakia, Lebanon, Romania, Lebanon, and Syria. These consist of eastern Christians who continue to observe the same customs and forms of worship as the Orthodox, but who accept papal primacy and are in full communion with the Holy See. They are often called 'Uniates', meaning those who accept the *Unia* or union with Rome. But this title tends to be used, especially by the Orthodox, with pejorative undertones; and so, like the terms 'Nestorian' and 'Monophysite', it is best avoided.

Distinct from the other Eastern Catholics are the Maronites in Lebanon, whose union with Rome dates back to the twelfth century, well before the Council of Florence. Here, then, is a fourth group within the complex tapestry of eastern Christendom. Alongside the three bodies already mentioned—the Church of the East, the Oriental Orthodox (non-Chalcedonian) and the Eastern Orthodox (Chalcedonian)—there exist also the Eastern Catholics. These last number today about 17 million.

Just as the schism between the Greek east and the Latin west did not occur as a single event, so also it did not have a single cause. Political and cultural factors played an important part. So also did questions of church order: for example, Greeks and Latins had different rules of fasting, and in the Eucharist the Greeks used (and still today use) leavened bread, whereas the Latins use unleavened bread or 'azymes'. More significantly, there are differences concerning marriage discipline. The Greeks allow remarriage after divorce, the Latins do not (but in the East no more than three marriages are permitted, whether after divorce or after the death of the other partner). In the Christian east the parish clergy are married men, fathers of families; although required to marry before being ordained, they continue after ordination to live with their wives in the usual way. It is only Orthodox bishops who, from the seventh century onwards, have had to be celibate (from the fourteenth century, if not earlier, it has been the practice for them to be not only celibate but in monastic vows, and this continues to be the rule today). In the Latin west, on the other hand, the clergy are unmarried, or at least have to be separated from their wives, although the rule of clerical celibacy was not strictly enforced until the eleventh century. Manifestly this question whether parish priests are married or celibate makes a radical difference to the relationship of the clergy to society.

However great the contribution of politics, culture, and church order to the gradual estrangement between East and West, these factors do not by themselves account for the separation. Doctrinal issues were also involved, and of these there are three in particular that call for mention. First, the two sides had divergent approaches to the state of the departed. The Greeks had reservations about the Latin doctrine of purgatory, as this was developed in the later medieval west, and in particular they disliked the practice of granting indulgences. But the disagreement here should not be exaggerated; both Orthodox and Catholics attach deep importance to prayer for the dead, and both would add that we cannot clearly explain how the faithful departed are helped by such prayers, although we are confident that they are.

More intractable are the two other issues, the *Filioque* and the papal claims. The Orthodox objected, and still object, to the way in which the west has added to the Creed. Whereas the original text of the Nicene-Constantinopolitan Creed (381) simply says that the Spirit 'proceeds from the Father', the west has inserted the further word *Filioque*, so that in the Latin version it is now stated that the Spirit 'proceeds from the Father *and the Son*'. Most western Christians today doubt whether this interpolation radically affects our understanding of the Spirit's person and work; but the Byzantines were convinced that it does. In any case they felt that the Latins had no right unilaterally to alter the Creed which is the common possession of the whole Christian world. As St Mark (Eugenicus) of Ephesus pleaded at the Council of Ferrara-Florence, 'This Symbol, this noble heritage of our Fathers, we demand back from you. Restore it then as you received it.'[14]

Alongside the *Filioque* there is also the problem of papal primacy. For Orthodoxy the pope is certainly the first bishop within an undivided Christendom, but he is *primus inter pares*, the first among equals. He is the elder brother within the Christian family, not a supreme ruler, and in particular he has no right to claim direct jurisdiction over the Christian east. In the words of another Greek spokesman at the Council of Ferrara-Florence, Archbishop Bessarion of Nicaea, 'Indeed, we are not ignorant of the rights and privileges of the Roman Church; but we know also the limits set to those privileges. . . . No matter how great the Roman Church is, it is notwithstanding less than an Ecumenical Council and the universal Church.'[15]

Today most people would regard the papal claims as the fundamental point at issue between Orthodoxy and Rome, but for the Byzantines the crucial matter was the *Filioque*. It is surprising (and illuminating) to note the relative importance ascribed to the three doctrinal questions at the Council of Ferrara-Florence, the last major occasion on which east and west have met at a common synod. Six months, with some interruptions, were spent discussing the addition of the *Filioque* to the Creed and the procession of the Holy Spirit. About two months were devoted to the subject of purgatory. But the papal claims occupied the participants for less than two weeks. Admittedly, that was right at the end of the Council, when everybody was anxious to go home.

Underlying specific questions such as purgatory, the *Filioque*, and papal primacy, there is also a further difficulty, far less precise and clear-cut. The Greek east and the Latin west came to have different understandings of the nature of theology, of the way in which religious thinking and discourse should be formulated. In comparison with Latin scholasticism, Orthodox theology has always been less dependent on juridical categories, less systematic, less confident about the use of reason and logic; in a word, more mystical. To quote a Greek patriarch of Jerusalem, Nektarios, writing in the mid-seventeenth century:

You have expelled, so it seems to us, the mystical element from theology. . . . In your theology there is nothing that lies outside speech or beyond the scope of inquiry, nothing wrapped round with silence and guarded by piety; everything is discussed. . . . There is no cleft in the rock to confine you when you confront the spectacle on which none may gaze; there is no hand of the Lord to cover you when you contemplate his glory (cf. Exod. 33: 22–23).[16]

This is not altogether fair to the Latin west, which has always possessed a rich and creative mystical tradition, but it indicates the reservations felt by many Orthodox about what they see as western 'rationalism'.

II: DEVELOPMENT

Limited first on its eastern border by the separation of the non-Chalcedonians, and then on its western border by the gradual estrangement with Rome, Byzantine Christianity expanded to the north. From the middle of the ninth century onwards, the patriarchate of Constantinople embarked upon an ambitious and for the most part highly successful programme of missionary work among the Slav peoples. Around 863 Patriarch Photius sent to Moravia (approximately the modern Czech Republic) two brothers from Thessalonica, Cyril and Methodius, known in the Orthodox tradition as the 'Illuminators of the Slavs'. In Moravia itself their mission met with only temporary success, and the Christianization of that land was taken over by German clergy owing allegiance to the Latin west. But elsewhere the initiative of Cyril and Methodius and of their disciples bore lasting fruit, leading to the conversion of Bulgaria and Serbia in the ninth century, and of Russia from the tenth century onwards. These three nations became in this way permanent members of the Orthodox family of churches.

From the start Orthodox missionary work outside the boundaries of the Byzantine Empire adopted as a basic principle the use of the vernacular in church worship. In contrast to western Europe, where Latin was everywhere employed as the liturgical language, the Byzantine missionaries translated the Scriptures and the service books into the language of the people, Slavonic. The native Slavs were quickly ordained to the priesthood and in due course also to the episcopate. This use of Slavonic led to the emergence in the Slav lands of local churches which were strongly national in character, and which in due course asserted their independence from the jurisdiction of the patriarchate of Constantinople, although in Russia this did not happen until the middle of the fifteenth century.

In what is now Romania, a national church emerged more

slowly than in Bulgaria, Serbia, and Russia. Here in fact Christianity dates back, long before the time of Cyril and Methodius, to the period of the Roman occupation of Dacia during the second and third centuries. But it was not until the late seventeenth century that the Romanian language began to be used in the church services, while a fully independent Romanian church was not established until the nineteenth century. It is often forgotten that the Romanian church—which, after the church of Russia, is the largest Orthodox church today—is neither Greek nor Slav but predominantly Latin in its language and culture. It should be seen as an expression not so much of *eastern* as of *occidental* Orthodoxy.

The Slav and Romanian churches, while profoundly influenced by Byzantine Christianity, at the same time came each to affirm the Orthodox faith in a form that was characteristically their own. This is true pre-eminently of Russia. Although it was not until the middle of the nineteenth century that Russian Orthodoxy began to produce original theologians such as Alexis Khomiakov, from its first beginnings it proved richly creative in the realm of spirituality. A notable feature of Russian religious life during the Kievan period (tenth to thirteenth centuries) was its kenotic outlook, its devotion to the humiliated Christ, its compassionate spirit, and its emphasis upon non-violence. 'Above all things,' wrote Prince Vladimir Monomakh (1053–1125) in his *Instruction* to his sons, 'forget not the poor, but support them to the extent of your means. Give to the orphan, protect the widow, and permit the mighty to destroy no man. Take not the life of the just or the unjust, nor permit him to be killed. Destroy no Christian soul, even though he be guilty of murder.'[17]

There emerged within Russian Christianity a new class of saints not found in the early Church or Byzantium: the Passion-Bearers. Here the pioneers were the two brothers Boris and Gleb. In 1015, following the death of their father St Vladimir, the first Christian ruler of Russia, they were murdered by their elder brother Sviatopolk. They could have offered resistance, but refused to take up arms in self-defence, preferring to avoid bloodshed. As Gleb says in the ancient *Life* of the two saints, 'It is better that I alone should die rather than such a multitude of souls.' They anticipated Mahatma Gandhi's teaching, 'If blood be shed, let it be our blood.' They were not martyrs in the strict sense, since they did not die for the Christian faith but as victims in a political conflict. Yet their innocent suffering was seen as a participation in Christ's Passion, and so they were given the title 'Passion-Bearers'. Significantly, they were the first saints to be glorified by the Russian church.

Russia has always been a land of extremes, marked by cruelty and violence, but also by gentleness and humble compassion. The suffering of the innocent and the defence-less, especially in the case of children—and Gleb was still a child when he died—is deeply valued by Russian Orthodoxy.

III: DEIFICATION

Having spoken about outward divisions and missionary development, let us now look more closely at the inner life of Orthodox Christianity. What might we single out as its distinctive characteristic, its dominant *leitmotif*, during the middle and late Byzantine eras (from, say, the seventh to the fifteenth centuries)? Among several possibilities, let us concentrate upon one only: deification—salvation and sanctification, that is to say, understood as 'divinization' or *theosis*, as a participation in the divine life (cf. 2 Pet. 1: 4). There was during these centuries a deepening awareness of the meaning of holiness, an increasing sense of the manner in which the sacred penetrates into the daily experience of the Christian. This can be seen in two ways: first, in the dispute about icons which lasted, with some intermissions, from 726 until 843; and secondly, in the evolution of mystical theology during the eleventh and more particularly the fourteenth century.

The Iconoclast Controversy was ostensibly a disagreement about religious art. How far is it legitimate, the contestants asked, to have icons in our churches and homes? (By an 'icon' is meant any representation of Christ, the Mother of God, the angels and the saints, whether in the form of mosaic, fresco, painted wooden panel, metal, embroidery, or from some other material.) If so, may these icons be venerated? Are they to be seen, not simply as pieces of decoration, but as channels of divine grace, endued with sacramental power? Can we show liturgical honour to images, and yet avoid falling into the sin of idolatry? To all these questions the seventh and last of the Ecumenical Councils, the second Council of Nicaea (787), answered confidently with a resounding *Yes*.

It may be doubted, however, whether the Iconoclast Controversy was exclusively or even primarily an argument about religious art. Almost certainly the dispute did not have a single cause. Some modern scholars see it as a debate about imperial ideology, about the place of the emperor within society and within the church; but, for myself, I wonder whether this was the main point at issue. During the eighth and ninth centuries, on the other hand, most contestants on either side, whether iconoclast or iconophile, regarded the conflict as a continuation of earlier controversies about the person of Christ; and they accused each other of being, in varying ways, either Nestorians (dividing the one Christ into two) or Eutychians (compromising the full integrity of Christ's human nature). In retrospect, these mutual accusations seem forced and unconvincing. Both sides in the Iconoclast Controversy accepted the Christological teaching of the first six Ecumenical Councils, and in particular they both upheld the Chalcedonian definition concerning Christ as a single person existing in two complete natures, without separation and without confusion.

If the Iconoclast Controversy was not primarily a debate concerning religious art, nor yet concerning imperial ideology or Christology, then what was it really about? Perhaps the most helpful line of approach—and here I come to my *leitmotif,* deification—is to see it as fundamentally a dispute about the position of the holy within Byzantine society. This is the opinion of Professor Peter Brown among others.[18] Among the questions raised by the controversy were these: Who controls the holy? How far should the divine be allowed to impinge upon the human world? Can the holy be narrowly restricted under the control of the emperor and the church hierarchy? Or does it spill out more unpredictably—we might even say, more untidily—into every aspect of human life?

The iconoclasts wished to confine the sphere of divine 'interference'—to use Dr Sebastian Brock's term[19]—to certain specific areas where the clergy were in full control, such as the Eucharist; and they argued that icons could not be holy because no specific prayer of blessing had been said over them.[20] The iconophiles saw matters differently. In their eyes, no specific human initiative is needed in order to bring something into the realm of the holy, for all that God has created is by its very nature intrinsically sacred. The whole world is a sacrament of the divine presence; the realm of matter in its entirety—wood, stone, earth, fire, air, water, the human body—is capable of being transfigured and glorified by the power of the Spirit.

St John of Damascus (*c.*655–*c.*750), the chief defender of the holy icons during the first stage of the controversy, repeatedly insisted on the holiness of matter. He based his argument in a simple and straightforward way—without invoking technical points concerning Nestorianism and Euty-chianism—upon the fact of Christ's incarnation. As God's creation, all material things are holy, and this intrinsic holiness was reaffirmed when God at his human birth took a material body:

Of old the incorporeal and formless God was not depicted at all; but now, since God has appeared in the flesh and come to dwell among humankind, I make an icon of God in so far as he has become visible. I do not worship matter but I worship the Creator of matter, who for my sake has become material, who has been pleased to dwell in matter, and who through matter has effected my salvation. . . . I salute all matter with reverence, for it is filled with divine energy and grace. . . . Do not insult matter, for it is not without honour; nothing is without honour that God has made. . . . The Word made flesh has deified the flesh.[21]

Following out John's line of thought, we may even say that Christians are the only true materialists, for they alone ascribe to matter its full potentiality for divinization.

In the centuries that follow the Iconoclast Controversy, the themes of deification and of the Spirit-bearing capacity of all material things—especially the human body—come once again to the fore in the mystical theology of St Symeon the New Theologian (959–1022) and of St Gregory Palamas (1296–1359), the protagonist of the Hesychast party during the mid-fourteenth century.[22] Both Symeon and Palamas are 'experiential' theologians, who believe that it is possible for human beings to attain, even in this present life, a meeting face to face with the risen Christ, and a direct and conscious experience of the indwelling Holy Spirit. This meeting and this experience, so they affirm, take the form more especially of a vision of divine light. The radiant glory beheld by the saints during prayer is not a merely physical light, although it may sometimes be seen through the physical eyes, nor is it something transitory and created; but it is nothing less than the supranatural light of Tabor which shone from Christ at his transfiguration. It is, according to Palamas, a manifestation of the eternal and uncreated energies of the Holy Trinity.

The light of Tabor is communicated not only to our souls but also to our bodies and, indeed, to the whole of the material creation. The divine energies are everywhere present and fill everything. Palamas and the fourteenth-century Hesychasts, like the iconophiles six hundred years earlier, are thus much concerned with the spiritual potentialities of material things, with the divine presence in every part of the natural world, with the holiness of the total cosmos. John of

Damascus, Symeon, and Palamas may in this way be seen as ecological theologians, which gives them a particular relevance to our present age. They affirm with William Blake, 'Every thing that lives is Holy'; and they would have added that everything that exists is also in some sense alive. The universe is not dead particles but living Presence.

There is always a danger in Christianity that mysticism may become divorced from the sacramental life of the church. On the whole this has not happened in the Orthodox east. Symeon and Palamas both stress the importance of holy communion, and Palamas's contemporary St Gregory of Sinai (d. 1346) defines mystical prayer as nothing else than 'baptism made manifest'.[23] There exists a long series of Byzantine commentaries on the Divine Liturgy by, for example, Dionysius the Areopagite, Maximus the Confessor, Germanus of Constantinople (d. 730), Nicolas of Andida (eleventh century), and above all Nicolas Cabasilas (*c.*1322–*c.*1391), and Symeon of Thessalonica (d. 1429). 'By this sacrament', writes Cabasilas of the Eucharist, 'we are made "flesh of his flesh, and bone of his bone" (Gen. 2: 23). . . . See in what sense the Kingdom of heaven is within us!'[24] For the Byzantines the Divine Liturgy is the supreme expression of the mystical life, the meeting-point between time and eternity, between this world and the next; it is, to use a phrase beloved of Orthodoxy, 'heaven on earth'.

Writers such as Symeon the New Theologian, Gregory Palamas, and Nicolas Cabasilas make one thing abundantly clear. Eastern Christianity during the later centuries of the Byzantine era was by no means somnolent or ossified, but it remained on the contrary intensely alive, dynamic and creative.

The Byzantines were indeed deeply traditionalist; but at its best the teaching which they upheld never ceased to be a *living* tradition.

So I come to the end of my song in a bottle. If you are not satisfied, then like the audience at the London theatre two-and-a-half centuries ago you can break up the furniture and start a bonfire in the street outside. But as a lover of Byzantine ceremonial and liturgical order I shall be happier if you do not.

5

THE LATER MIDDLE AGES

Alexander Murray

We live in a time of zeal for standardizing terms, like weights and measures, or even the word 'chocolate'. The enthusiasm has not got as far as medieval history, happily, so that the 'High Middle Ages' can mean quite different periods in Germany and Italy, and two books I know in English say they are about the 'Central Middle Ages', but cover periods two centuries apart. We can all think of examples. So let me just say that this lecture, following the elegant carpentry of the series, will cover western Christianity between 1000 and 1500. Perhaps, though, I should add a word to say why I expressed happiness just now, not scandal, at the confusion of medieval terminology.

My reason is that medieval terms easily become tyrants, given half a chance. Take our own subject. The years 1000 to 1500 include most of the things we think of as characteristic of medieval Christianity: the Crusades, scholasticism, the Gothic, and more like that. I might fairly be expected to make my lecture a set of vignettes on these things. The problem is that all those words—Crusades, scholasticism, the Gothic—were coined after the Middle Ages, or at least (as to the Crusades) well after what they purported to describe. That is true of most front-rank medieval terminology, including 'feudalism' and (above all, of course) 'medieval' itself. *Medium aevum* was another Renaissance neologism. Far from thinking they were in the middle of anything, medieval people—if they thought about it at all—either imagined they were living near the *end* of everything (for better or worse), or that the Roman Empire was still going on and nothing had changed, or perhaps—a few, sometimes—that *they* were the renaissance. Certainly not the middle. In other words you and I can hardly open our mouths about the Middle Ages without anachronism. Most of the anachronisms are traceable to the Renaissance and Reformation, flexibly understood. The fact that those last two terms *were* contemporary with what they denote helps identify the source of all the contamination. When we talk about the Middle Ages we are all Renaissance men (or women), or Reformation (ditto).

To escape these conventional anachronisms, in approaching Christianity from 1000 to 1500, I shall adopt an unconventional one, and invite you to come up with me in a space-satellite—of the kind used to monitor weather in the Atlantic—and see the whole subject from there. Whoosh! Up we go. And what do we see, looking down on little Christendom, over those five centuries? (Now we are up here I recall it is not so anachronistic: Dante imagined himself doing precisely this, around 1300, looking down from the stars of *Paradiso*.) What we see is something so big and obvious it is easily missed at ground level: between 1000 and 1500 Latin Christendom had doubled in size, and quadrupled in population. In size, first: to prove it, Fig. 3 shows a satellite photograph to indicate the doubling—or almost doubling: perhaps I mean one and three quarters. The fourfold rise in population comes in a lot of tiny blobs we can just see from our satellite (but could not get in the photograph because the weather was too cloudy). The blobs might be lit up at night by the occasional bonfire or even the blobs be themselves on fire (it happened horribly often), their lanterns and candles being too faint to see from up there. So they are just visible, with a strain. I refer to towns, which in these five centuries expanded and multiplied faster than Christendom. Not every medieval town mushroomed like Florence, whose population *quin*tupled in the two centuries after 1100, or Paris, which may have matched or exceeded that. A few little towns even disappeared, and all of them, big or little, suffered population hiccups, especially severe at the Black Death and just afterwards (when plague returned). But they grew again. By 1500, taking Latin Christendom as a whole, it can safely be said—and was said in this very hall, by George Holmes in his inaugural lecture as Chichele Professor[1]—that there would have been no Renaissance or Reformation if the towns had not by then become the swelling, thrusting, self-confident adolescents they were—their more fortunate burghers living (to quote Aeneas Silvius Piccolomini, on visiting Nuremberg) 'like kings of Scotland'.

Expansion, then, and urbanization. These are what are visible from our satellite. My aim in this lecture is to show the ways in which these big changes, in the macrocosm of western Christianity, affected the microcosm, individual people, in the

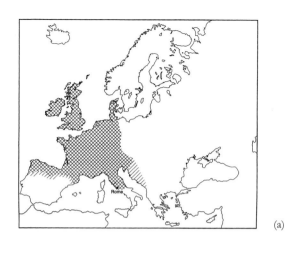

(a)

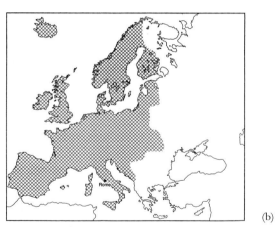

(b)

Figure 3. The expansion of Latin Christendom in the Later Middle Ages.
(a) Late tenth century   (b) Late fifteenth century

99

way they understood and practised their religion. So let me start at once with the expansion; or rather, one half of it. The expansion roughly splits into that north and south of the Alps. The two processes had different characters and effects, and are best dealt with separately. Since the southern effects were more immediate, I will start with that, go on with the towns, and finish with the northward expansion, the reasons for that strange order becoming clear (I hope) as we go.

The south, then. First, the basic data. In Provence in the year 1000, people still not on crutches could remember how a saintly abbot of Cluny, head of the most revered monastic family in Christendom, had been kidnapped and held to ransom while crossing the Alps, by Saracens. The Saracens in the case were freebooters of a kind left over from a war which had been going on more or less since the birth of Islam, and had mostly gone in its favour, leaving two and a half sides of the Mediterranean coastlands in Muslim hands, and all the western Mediterranean islands, including (from 827) Sicily— from where a force had come up in 845 and sacked St Peter's. Neighbouring Christian land was exposed to raids, often for slaves. Modern Italy still keeps record of those years with place names like 'Punta Saracena', 'Monte Saraceno', and just 'Saracino'. Around the year 1000 Christians began to turn the tables. In Spain the Reconquest had begun in earnest in the ninth century, heartened by what medieval language called the 'discovery' of the body of the Apostle James, at what became thereby 'Sant Iago'. But it was only after *c.*1050 the great leap forward came. Christian advances pushed the boundary steadily southwards, to take in Seville in 1248, including the Balearics *en route*, and leaving only Granada in its mountains, to fall in 1492. Sardinia and Corsica had long ago succumbed to Italian fleets first sent in 1016, while in the south, by 1091 William the Conqueror's Norman cousins brought southern Italy and Sicily into the Latin Christian camp. What we call the First Crusade, in 1096, extended to the eastern Mediterranean a reconquest which had already turned the western part back into a Christian lake. From an Italian business perspective, the daring deeds of Richard the Lionheart and his like, in defending the Christian Holy Land, had this considerable asset value, that they admitted Italian ships to eastern seas, and thence to Egyptian, Syrian, and above all to Byzantine, ports, and all beyond.

In the west, most of that southwards expansion remained constant, its setbacks temporary. But in the long run Latin Christian power in the south proved to be like an eiderdown, slipping askew on a Mediterranean bed. While it brought Spain cosily into Christendom, it left the east exposed. The long-term contraction of the eastern frontier was directly the work of the Turks. On first meeting this Steppe people, in mutual slaughter, in Anatolia in 1097, the Frankish crusaders had said the Turks were the finest people in the world *except* for the Franks, and would be as good as the Franks if only they (the Turks) were Christian. But they were not. The Turks were recent converts to Islam, who took fairly literally its urgings to get up and go in spreading the faith, and in the 1060s, as the Seljuks (a Turkish tribe), had burst into the wealthy Byzantine province of Anatolia, turning it thenceforth into Turkey. A second-burst wave of pressure, from a different branch of Turks, came north in the thirteenth century from the Egyptian Mamluks, who ended the Christian kingdom in Palestine; and in the aftermath of that, a third wave, the Ottomans, moved up from Syria, forming a gradually rising tide around fortress Constantinople. When Constantinople was finally submerged in 1453, they went on to conquer the Balkans, bite pieces out of Hungary, and even, for one terrifying year (1480), occupy Otranto in southern Italy. The image of an eiderdown, slipping skew on a bed, is too homely to convey the character of this process. It often involved the massacre of the population of the whole town. (The Ottomans who took Otranto cut its archbishop in half.)

This lecture is supposed to be about Christian*ity*. So far it has been all about Christen*dom*. Actually a single medieval Latin word, *Christianitas*, covered both concepts. Another time we could brood on that. But now it is best to distinguish them, and ask what results these changes in Christen*dom* had on the way people understood and practised Christian*ity*. Let me begin with a word on the Bible. I may not have been listening carefully enough at school, but I think I was taught that medieval churchmen were not interested in the Bible. It was Beryl Smalley who was most responsible for dissolving this myth. She showed—it was obvious once she had said it—that they were barely interested in anything else. Most writings by medieval divines were commentaries or meditations on, digests of, or selections from the Bible, or systematic treatments of questions arising (which got its own name as the new science of theology, *c.*1120).[2] There is a problem with the Bible, as with all written authority. It is best explained by an analogy. At the oculist's, a test you can take for colour-blindness employs a booklet, whose pages are printed with coloured dots, which form numbers, like '62', or '41'. But the dots have been printed in subtly different shades, so that if you are colour-blind, and see (say) reds as blues, you will read '62' as '25', or whatever. The oculist can tell from what numbers you read what your eyes are like. That is, the same dots produce different readings, depending on conditions in our cognitive mechanism. It is exactly like that with the Bible. The same marks on the page can produce different readings, according to the traditions, circumstances, and dispositions of the people reading it. This is not to say there is no right way. There is a right number to be read in those dots. Reading the right number in the Bible is vastly harder because it concerns more than digits and physical colours; but for the Bible to have any authority at all we must believe there is a right way. Finding it is partly what the church (however we understand it) is for.

The extension of medieval Latin Christendom southwards, then, had two main effects on the way Christians understood their Bible. One concerned war. To say that the southern Christian frontier extended by war and the northern by diplomacy would be to oversimplify. Readers of Richard Fletcher's recent book, *The Conversion of Europe*, will know the wide variety of ways in which peoples of the north and north-east came into Christianity: brute force just occasionally came into it and often hovered in the background, as it does in most diplomacy. But the contrast remains, because in the south, force was normal; it was the way Christendom expanded.

Nor is the contrast accidental. In the north, Christendom advanced against societies less developed than itself, economically and politically, whose pagan rulers usually ended up by realizing, despite jealousies and conservatisms, that Christianity offered what *Which?* magazine would call the 'best buy'. They joined what they could not beat. The south was different because, in facing Islam, Christianity was up against something not unlike itself. For all their dark faces, strange babble, and boundlessly impertinent religious self-confidence (not to mention sexual licence, according to popular lore), the Arab world had a religion which informed Christians knew was related to their own. It deserved respect. Listen to Pope Gregory VII on the subject, writing to a North African emir in early 1076. The emir had sent a candidate for consecration as bishop, to look after the emir's Christian subjects. In returning his courtesy, Gregory said the emir's acts bore the unmistakable mark of divine charity, the most important of all human qualities:

God, who wishes all men to be saved and none to perish, sets no human quality at a higher value than charity, one towards another, so that no-one should do to others what he would not have done to himself.

Christians and Muslims, especially, owed this charity to each other:

This charity is something your people and ours owe each other more especially than other peoples, since both of us, albeit in different ways [*licet diverso modo*], believe in one God, worshipping him each day as creator and sustainer of the universe.[3]

Like many debts of mutual charity this one was not always paid. Two years earlier the same pope had called on Christian knights from all over Latin Christendom to form a military expedition to fight *against* Muslims. The occasion was a Byzantine 'SOS', reporting that unbelievers—*pagani*, meaning those Seljuk Turks—had invaded Anatolia and 'massacred many thousands of Christians as if they were sheep'. The sheep had included the emperor, Romanus IV, killed with many others at the battle of Manzikert in 1071. Now, the SOS said that Constantinople itself was threatened, and there could be no guarantee that this bulwark of Christendom would not fall.[4] Gregory's letter on the subject is dated 1074. It marks the birth of the idea to be realized twenty-one years later as the First Crusade.

In the Gospel, when Jesus was about to be arrested by the Temple police, St Peter drew his sword and cut off the ear of one of the police. Jesus told Peter to put up his sword, healed the ear, and submitted to arrest. Pacifism has been said to be, if not *the* heart, then *near* the heart of Christianity. It is fair to ask how, in the face of a monotheism known to be like-minded, Christians came to interpret their Bible in a way which sanctioned war. It is a long story, with a huge literature. The classic remains Carl Erdmann's *The Origin of the Idea of Crusade*, its stature all the greater for its having been published in Germany in the Nazi period (in 1935, to be exact); and you cannot tell—unless it is in the author's intuition—that it was the entry of Germanic personnel into the top ranks of the church, after Henry III's reform of the papacy in 1045, that brought with it into the church the spirit of Wotan, the old Germanic god. That may be part of the picture. But Erdmann knew, and wrote, that there were other parts. As a more recent contribution to the literature, B. Z. Kedar's *Crusade and Mission*, makes even clearer, in every century concerned, from the eighth to the fifteenth, Christians expressed a wide range of views on war, for and against and with innumerable conditions and reservations—not, in fact, generically unlike the views expressed on nuclear weapons in our own day. The war party did not neglect their Bible, but read it in a non-pacifist sense. The story of Christ's telling Peter to put up his sword, for instance, showed that his disciple must have been carrying a sword in the first place. It is easy to find other New Testament texts (like a miracle for a centurion), which appear to legitimize armed force in some circumstances, to say nothing of the Old Testament.

Old Germanic spirits apart, the way contemporary divines read these texts was influenced by two distinct factors: doctrinal inheritance, and current circumstance. The doctrinal inheritance reflected the entire course of Christian history so far. Christianity had not made its own political frontiers. The pagan Caesars had done that, before Christ came on the scene, by creating the Roman empire, both helped and hindered by the warring Jewish kings of the Old Testament. Christians had nothing to do with it. For the first three centuries, the only connection Christians had with state coercion was to suffer from it, with a patience heroic enough to make it the central core of the Christian historical tradition, celebrated daily in liturgical references to martyrs. Then came a change. At the beginning of the fourth century the Emperor Constantine became a Christian, and empire and Christianity became (as it were) married. Each party had to come to terms with the other. On the Christian side this meant a reappraisal of the legitimate functions of government, including war so long as it was 'just'. One historical current even went back and justified Roman conquests in retrospect, seeing them as part of God's plan, preparing for Christianity, like the Old Testament. The marriage of Christianity and empire lasted three more centuries, until the political empire fell finally to bits in the late sixth century. By that time the double Christian inheritance on war had been imprinted on, among other texts later held authoritative, Justinian's codifications of Roman law, to serve as a quarry for medieval jurists.

This double inheritance passed down to Gregory VII and his supporters, and they tilted it further on the side of war. This was due to the second factor, circumstance. Some of the circumstances were those of domestic politics, such as bishops' peace-keeping role, and papal–imperial rivalry. The most important circumstance nevertheless concerned the frontier, and Islam. A historical difference between Christianity and Islam was that the latter *had* had to build its own political frontiers. Muhammad's revelations had come at the heart of a polytheistic society; he was persecuted, and obliged to flee, in 622, from Mecca to Medina, where his movement had to defend itself with arms, and did so with a success which exploded, in the three generations after Muhammad's death in 632, to subdue a huge strip of Eurasia and North Africa. The western end of the strip happened to include most of the southern section of the Christian Roman empire. Politically, around 1000, Christians were therefore on the back foot in respect of Islam, and, being historically-minded, knew they were—whether or not they thought it realistic, or in accordance with their particular interpretation of Christianity, to do anything about it. The histories of the two traditions meant that Muslims had a shorter doctrinal distance to travel to sanction 'just' war. They too, it is true, with their idea of *jihad*, or holy war, gave it a range of interpretations. But necessarily, given the history of the two traditions, Islam lived nearer to the military end of it, as exemplified by those Seljuks. The eleventh-century confrontation between Christianity and Islam, as tables began to turn, moved Christianity in the same direction.

The rise of military ethic was one change in Christianity, brought about by its southern expansion. The second change concerned organization and law, and in particular a rise in Roman authority. This change, too, arose out of long-term developments. It was once generally agreed that the Roman empire had collapsed in the fifth century, with the Germanic invasions. In 1935 the Belgian historian Henri Pirenne turned medieval historiography upside-down by re-dating the end of the 'Romanitas', as he called it, to the eighth century, because (he argued) only then was its underlying economy destroyed. That underlying economy had depended on trade across the Mediterranean. Romans had called the Mediterranean *mare nostrum*, 'our sea', and their monetary economy, towns, and cosmopolitan culture were all connected with that trade. These features lasted while the trade survived, and when it stopped, they stopped. It was halted, Pirenne said, not by a handful of impressionable Germans, but by those Muslim invasions of the seventh and eighth centuries, which put half the Mediterranean in the hands of a rival, self-confident culture, numerous and linguistically incomprehensible.

Pirenne's theory is almost as old as I am. It has been through wars, and been somewhat mutilated. But the fact that students of the period still have to master it is just one sign (among some more cogent ones) that the core of his intuition was sound: that Mediterranean trade was a fundamental factor, and that it declined. That is enough to explain how Pirenne can help us now. After the millennium, Italian cities advanced into the Mediterranean again, reviving its trade. On Pirenne's theory the following century should see a return of the Roman empire. Behold! There it is, rising up out of the water again, except that this time (as happens when once-living organisms have been long under water), it could only come up as a ghost, in person of the Roman papacy.

You may say that economic explanation for the Gregorian reform is in need of hard facts on the ground, and it could certainly find some: for instance, the pension of 1000 gold dinars *per annum*, doubled in 1077, paid by the conquering kings of Castile to Cluny; or (again) the connections we know existed between the reformers in several Italian cities and new business interests. But we are in a space-satellite. The coincidence is too big to be missed, and only invites us, after noting it, to turn to that ghost, the spiritual Roman empire of the Gregorian papacy, and identify its main characteristics.

The first concerned the bishops of Rome. Their claims to ecclesiastical primacy were old, but had new emphasis. In biblical terms, the pattern of dots which now achieved greater prominence was Matthew 16: 18, Christ's commission to St Peter, interpreted as applying to all the bishops of Rome, a text which lay at the base of a formidable doctrinal armoury, employed by Gregory VII and his supporters. About a generation after his death, the Italian revival enhanced Roman primacy further, this time *via* Bologna. There, around 1140, Gratian's *Decretum* assembled a new synthesis of canon law, the legal fabric that held the Church together as *societas Christiana*. To fill the many gaps in existing canon law, Gratian had recourse to Roman imperial law, then recently rediscovered. Roman law tended to unify canon law, and to underline the sovereignty of the supreme appellate judge, in old Rome 'the prince', in the new, the bishop of Rome. Granted the unique level of sophistication which canon law enjoyed in the twelfth century, this feature could not fail to raise the papacy even higher. It was the ghost not only of Augustus the conqueror, but also of Justinian the lawgiver.

The emergence of this ghostly Roman empire had an impact in European history hard to overestimate. In terms of hard politics its most important consequence was that no other, more purely political, heir to the Roman empire could establish itself on European soil. The foremost candidates were the German 'Roman Emperors'. For half our period, until around 1250, they tried to do so, adding the word 'Holy' to their title, in 1157, to show their empire was as holy as the pope's. But their imperial claim dragged them into Italian politics which, with the popes' active connivance, proved too damaging and expensive. So after 1250, by stages and degrees, the German kings at last recognized the Alps as a suitable southern boundary, and turned their attention to the better long-term investments to be had in their eastern borderlands, where they became successful colonial princes. Two centuries of papal–imperial conflict had left the papacy damaged as well as the empire, but had, politically, one overwhelmingly significant long-lasting result, still with us. In the critical phase of its state-formation, western Europe developed as a plurality of states with a common ideology, rather than as one semi-sacred superstate, of the kind common in other times and places of world history.

That was the most direct political consequence. The cultural fruits of the ghostly Roman Empire were equally pregnant. Like most cultural endeavours this one had to depend on an elite (Greek: *klērikos*), the clergy. The reformers' council of 1059, the same which made the election of the pope a matter for churchmen alone, was important for the clergy because it revived an old rule that priests should be celibate: a rule observed widely enough—despite its chronic breaches—to ensure the establishment of a universal, Latin-speaking group abstracted from ordinary society, and simultaneously bound to each other by laws peculiar to themselves (the literal meaning of 'privilege': 'private law'). Among other advantages offered by the celibacy rule—as Sir Richard Southern observed with characteristic lucidity in his recent book *Scholastic Humanism and the Unification of Europe*—was that it gave the Gregorian church a decisive selling-point to the lay nobility, for whom priestly celibacy did some of the services of birth-control, protecting dynastic estates.

A strengthening in the ecclesiastical profile of Rome, and of a Latin-speaking clerical elite, combined to raise this new ghostly empire. Of the main consequences of its rise, I shall distinguish three. The first, a domestic resonance of that militarism abroad, was the persecution of its outlaws. In his *The Formation of a Persecuting Society* (Oxford, 1987), R. I. Moore has argued that as twelfth-century western Europeans became more self-consciously Christian—as distinct from staying absorbed in local and ethnic loyalties—a harsher light fell on those in some way *not* Christian, like Jews, and, above all, heretics, and that they were accordingly noticed and persecuted with growing zeal, and often with violence. The kernel of that argument is sound, though we should not forget that the violence was not an invention of ecclesiastical lawyers, whose law, taken as a whole, was the principal contemporary influence tending to reduce violence. The violence itself was age-old and endemic, including extreme forms such as the burning-alive of individuals thought to house evil spirits. What the churchmen did, and only at the extreme outer edge of their measures to ostracize heretics, was to channel the violence in order to build a cortex round the church's identity, to protect it like the prickles on a porcupine. This applies especially to the heresy-inquisition, created after the war against the Albigensian heretics in 1231. The *inquisitio* was a standard Roman law procedure for the public prosecution of crime. It was on the march anyway during the thirteenth century as part of the build-up of secular principalities. Church leaders wanted a procedure to ensure the 'right' people got persecuted, after the hit-and-miss massacres of the Albigensian war.

Meanwhile, in the porcupine protected by those quills, the Roman-led clerical church produced two less spectacular but more substantial results. One concerns education. The learning of Latin ('grammar', whence our 'grammar schools') was not only encouraged by authorities from above, needing educated staff, but was desired from below by young people with an eye on the job-market. So the schools swelled, not only throwing up new entities like the University of Oxford, but subtly, over the generations, transforming the content of education, to produce surprising paradoxes. Some arose through the fortunes of Latin itself. In the first century of the reform, the church pushed hard enough for the universality of its language to kill off budding vernaculars, like Anglo-Saxon. Once that universality had been achieved, Latin could become a vehicle for radically anti-clerical treatises—as had happened certainly by the fourteenth century. Another Latin paradox was the absorption by Christian scholars of the pagan thought of antiquity. The more effort a clerk put into his perfection of the church's language, the more exposed he was to the ideas of its paragons like Cicero and Seneca. Pagan philosophy is like a sea, gently lapping against the shore of scholastic thought and occasionally overflowing it. That did not have to wait for the fifteenth-century Florentine Renaissance. The conditions were there from Gregory VII on. If I am allowed yet another kind of paradox, it is one concerning certain supernatural beliefs. From time immemorial some people had believed in the kind of witch who flies round at night. In the twelfth century, respectable clerical opinion scorned the belief as a pagan old wives' tale. But more and more people got access to literate culture, which consequently moved in their direction, and by 1486 the Dominican authors of the notorious witch-hunting manual, *Malleus maleficarum* ('The Hammer of Witches') could treat a belief in flying witches as all but an article of faith.

Persecution; education; that leaves one more of my three consequences, big enough to be seen from the sky, of the rise of the ghostly Roman empire. It is the biggest, and can only be called Christianity, emphasis now on the *first* syllable. I mean by it what the Christian religion had that other kinds of monotheism did not, at the heart of their doctrine: a God who had come all the way down to humble earth and become man, for the sake of all who would accept him. This distinctively Christian focus is witnessed by both the intellectual and the practical aspects of the post-Gregorian church. In his book *The Papal Monarchy*—one I happen to disagree with about papal monarchy but applaud on everything else—Colin Morris describes twelfth-century theology as 'profoundly Christ-centred', and sees its image of Christ as that 'of the historical Jesus'. He gives supportive examples from ascetic monasticism and from popular devotion. From the first, we get treatises on the Five Wounds of Christ and other aspects of Jesus' life and death. In popular devotion, we find a growth in the use of the crucifix, in references to the Eucharist, and in the cult of Mary, spreading widely from the twelfth century. To Morris' assigning of the Marian cult to interest in the historical Jesus I would add a second, complementary explanation. As the church became more legalized, delinquent Christians might doubt about whose side Jesus was on. Was he siding with the bosses? Mary's miracles specialized in the really down-and-out, in need of the unconditional love of his mother. With her, you could be sure she was on your side.

The same emphasis on Christ is clear in academic theology. St Anselm of Canterbury's influential treatise *Cur Deus Homo*? ('Why did God become Man?'), written just before 1100, was only one of a series of treatises on the incarnation, some explicitly addressed to Jews (who did not accept it), some not. The same preoccupation can be detected in the repeated twelfth-century attempts to define the balance between the persons in the Trinity, not least when the creation of Trinity Sunday made some people think there must be a *fourth* person, namely the Trinity as a whole. The attempts came to a conclusion with the opening clause of the proceedings of the fourth Lateran Council in 1215, which consisted of a creed elaborated for this purpose.

That context is significant. If the ghostly Roman empire had a high point, the council of 1215 was it, following three others held in Rome's church of St John Lateran during the twelfth century. The 1215 council had the widest representation of any medieval council: more than a thousand prelates attended, from all corners of Christendom, and the character of its moving spirit, Innocent III, and of its detailed provisions, point in the same direction. As a young Italian nobleman Innocent had studied theology in Paris, in a generation when the Christ-centred theology taught there had burgeoned into what historians have dubbed the 'biblical-moral school'. This was a group of theologians—they included the English Stephen Langton, famous as a theologian even before he became archbishop of Canterbury—collectively noted for the focus they gave to the Bible's practical implications, in morals and politics, as in fields like trade, war, and criminal justice, and in family matters like marriage. This practical emphasis— the bringing the divine down to earth—struck root in the future pope's mind. After leaving Paris he wrote what would prove his most widely read book (over 140 manuscripts survive), on the Mass, whose central miracle, identified by the relatively new word 'transubstantiation', he compared to that of the incarnation, in that in both the divine came down into the world of flesh and blood.[5] It fits this background that

Innocent as pope should have established *Vicarius Christi* as principal papal title.

The seventy-one provisions of Innocent's council are a practical extension of what he had learned in Paris. Some are directed against heresy, or at barbarous superstition, like a clause which forbids priests from taking any further part in the judicial ordeal. One clause protects marriage from captious claims of consanguinity, then the main ground for divorce. The great majority of the clauses are designed simply to make the pastoral church function properly, with numerous stipulations about the education, selection, and discipline of clergy at all levels, and on the encouragement of public preaching of 'the divine word', and the confession of sins. The core of the council's thinking is betrayed best in one short phrase in canon no. 27: *Ars artium regimen animarum*: 'the right ordering of souls is the art of arts': its significance is confirmed, not weakened, when we know it came from the fourth-century Greek Father, St Gregory Nazianzen, by way of the ninth-century Carolingian reformers—who hover, in fact, like ancestral spirits, behind many of Innocent's reforming ideas.[6]

So much, then, for the results of Christian expansion to the south part of the first feature we saw from the space-satellite. Let secondly now turn to those blobs, the towns. I introduced Henri Pirenne a moment ago, with his theories on the late Roman empire, and he can help again. As the political power of the old Roman empire had retreated towards Constantinople, responsibility for western cities, including Rome, had fallen increasingly to their bishops, ruling from urban shells over their 'dioceses' (to use the term of imperial secular administration). The eleventh-century commercial recovery breathed new life into those cities, with some lasting effects. The first effect was to boost the rents of the bishops and their clergy, but that was not lasting, because it commercialized church office, and provoked the reaction that became Gregory VII's reform. I said earlier that the reform had the support of some of the newer business interests, and while the two movements needed each other that support endured. But the business interests soon struck out on their own, organized themselves as independent communes, and, in each city, set about relieving the local bishop of his vast inherited lands and jurisdictions.

In Italy this slimming-down of bishops occurred between about 1100 and 1300. We know it did because we can see the beginning and end of the process and just occasionally glimpses in between. We also see it, crystal-clear, in the back-to-front version of its main exception, Rome. Like other Italian bishops, the bishop of Rome had inherited huge secular jurisdictions. Unlike them, he now had a world-wide function, important enough to protect his jurisdiction from local rivals. The movement for a Roman commune constantly struggled for life, but its struggles always ended in violent deaths, like those of the scholar-revolutionary Arnold of Brescia in 1155, and of 'the Mussolini of the Middle Ages', Cola di Rienzo, in 1354. Rome's communal aspirations went on being a thorn in the pope's side, but thorns on their own do not kill people and, in the event, somehow, the papacy's early medieval structure lasted right on until 1870.

In northern Europe the same process would happen later, and at the behest this time of rising monarchies, not independent towns. But the monarchies were conscious of acting in alliance with their own, non-independent towns and conscious, too, that the Italians had got there first. The rule is again well-illustrated in its exception. In the north it was the big Rhineland archbishoprics whose dark-age structure endured deep into the modern period. This was because in the critical centuries of German development there *was* no strong national monarchy to slim them down, not least because the three biggest archbishops were imperial Electors, and saw to it that no monarchy got too strong (if any dynasty looked like going that way, the Electors changed the dynasty). So the old structures lasted on. Luther's aversion to the archbishop of Mainz had this background.

To see why this urban expropriation of bishops had its effect on Christian*ity*, let us go back to the Bible. The Gospel said Christ and his disciples were poor. Or it could say that; again there were texts, and texts. The argument went on that since bishops and clergy were *not* poor, their ministry was a usurpation. So they should be made poor. Throughout our period that argument issued from what historians have come to call the poverty movement. It should not always be taken at its word. The awful truth was that many bishops and clergy *were* poor, especially when dispossessors had finished with them. New-broom authorities were for ever having to make their subordinates keep accounts, to see that their churches were not poorer than they need be. And the fact that where bishoprics were poorest of all, in south-western France, the Albigensian heresy sprang up and flourished, is enough to alert us to a *trompe-l'œil* element in the poverty movement. Why it throve was not because it always spoke the objective truth, but because its message served as an ideological barrage for the dispossession of the bishops by the new urban interests. Most of the so-called heresies and their also-rans drew sustenance from this poverty movement, first in Italy (as in the scholar-revolutionary I mentioned, Arnold of Brescia), and later in the northern monarchies. The famous English heretic would be Wyclif, who demanded dispossession of the church. In 1377 his doctrines were condemned by an anxious pope as a re-run, 'with a few terms altered', of those of the great Italian dispossessor, Marsiglio of Padua.

To say that the poverty movement should not always be taken at its word is not to say it never should. The movement contained forms of religious expression with an authenticity beyond dispute. It was again Innocent III who made this distinction most decisively, by approving, after hesitation, the mission of St Francis of Assisi. In a lecture on medieval Christianity it may seem late in the day for me to mention its best-loved representative; but this is his place. We never would have heard of St Francis but for the order he founded, and we never would have heard of that but for the church, *with* its bishops, and especially the bishops of Rome, a whole series of whom took a keen personal interest in the order. Of the reasons why they did, I shall explain the most urgent.

It all arose from the papacy's constant, ongoing 'reform' programme, as embodied in the programmes of the Lateran councils. In practice, the success of that programme depended on a humble functionary, the parish priest. Parishes as such, as a geographical grid, dividing up Christendom, had more or less settled into place by about 1100. Each parish was to have its priest, celebrating, preaching, and hearing confessions.

That was in theory. But there were two problems, of quality and quantity. Of quality I could, but need not, say more than to mention Valerie Flint's book *The Rise of Magic in Early Medieval Europe*. If it is to be believed—incredible as it seems, the evidence is too abundant not to be—very many early medieval priests doubled as magicians (what else would they be doing 'blessing' the iron and water of the judicial ordeal?). Then, as to quantity. The year 1100, roughly the date when the parish grid was in place, was also roughly the date when the towns began to mushroom. Magician or otherwise, the urban priest had more souls on his hands than he could cope with. Nor did it help that, as if those two conditions were not enough, at the same moment the Gregorian reformers started demanding high standards and encouraging criticism of those who failed. We know from rare documented cases that these circumstances sometimes encouraged heresy, and can see that they must have done. There was a pastoral vacuum, which nature abhors. Efforts to fill it, by those Lateran councils, worked to some extent. We know for a fact there *were* good parish priests, despite the criticism. But we also know there were not nearly enough to support the structure that alone could realize the reformers' ideal.

It was here that St Francis entered the story: *he* came as a godsend. He was the *Poverello*, of course, and a godsend as that alone, his memory one of the lasting treasures of capitalist Europe. But I do not mean that. St Francis was a godsend to the pastoral church because he proved to be the starting-point of the mendicant orders (from *mendicare*, 'to beg'). He was not the only *poverello*, though others had different configurations of the ideal. At around the same time as Francis' mission, the learned Spanish clerk Dominic sold all his books, gave the money to charity, and directed his wits against the Albigensian heresy, gathering fellow-workers as he did so. His movement and that of St Francis influenced each other, one with its idealization of pure poverty, the other with its constitutional skill (where Dominicans were pioneers: the term 'friar', brother, for the mendicants deliberately freed them from simple hierarchy). By the middle of the thirteenth century the Franciscans and Dominicans had been joined by other orders, the Carmelites, Augustinian Friars, but several smaller orders, like the short-lived order of Brothers of the Sack, who lived in Oxford on the site which became the Eastgate Tavern.

East*gate*: it was on the edge of the then Oxford, and that was typical of mendicant orders. That was again intentional. Most friars' convents were near city perimeters not only because land was cheaper but because parish activity was thinner. Bishops and senior mendicants can be detected carefully planning the location of mendicant convents, in and between towns, matching mendicant provision to a town's population, like planning committees with supermarkets today. Their care helps betray its motive. The friars were a new kind of clergy, to meet the pastoral problem of the towns: group-practice clergy, like the group-practice General Practitioners who support our Health Service in a similar way. The advantages offered by the friars included their mutual support, in learning and discipline, and above all, low cost, since friars had no families to support, and made plain living a virtue. St Francis' strict poverty was soon modified. Within three generations most mendicant convents were receiving rents (the main form of productive investment, usury being forbidden: Oxford colleges lived on rents). Francis' portrait remained on the wall, for all that—metaphorically and sometimes literally—his memory a reminder, to all friars, that such modest property as they were allowed was to be used 'in the manner of the poor': *usus pauper*. There was nothing here to inspire jealousy from business interests. Quite the opposite: the merchants loved the friars. In a fund-raising sermon for Pisa's Franciscan convent in 1257, an archbishop drove his appeal home by saying, 'after all, St Francis *was* a merchant'. Neither he nor anyone else seems to have reflected that Francis *had* been a merchant, but had reacted diametrically against commercial ideals.

The old clergy were another matter. They *were* jealous, for both their status and their income. At first the old-style clergy picked what quarrels they could. Jean de Meung, author of the most widely-read of all medieval French vernacular poems, *The Romance of the Rose* (around 1283), lived almost next door to the Paris Dominicans. An old-style so-called 'secular' clerk, he could not abide the airs his neighbours gave themselves and poured his awesome talents into the creation of the most pungent of medieval satires, *Faux Semblant* ('False Seeming'), the Hypocrite, a barely-disguised caricature of a Dominican. *Faux Semblant* had honours in store, including that of being transposed bodily into *The Canterbury Tales*, as Chaucer's Pardoner. But satire is a reluctant tribute to success, and this was. By 1325, all mendicant orders together, in Europe as a whole, could count some 90,000 members, a quarter of them in the dependent women's orders.[7] The secular clergy were soon paying their tribute in a less ambivalent way, by buying, reading, and using, the books that poured from mendicant writers on a wide range of pastoral subjects, like, to take two of many scores of instances, those Dominican best-sellers (each surviving in hundreds of manuscripts) Guillaume Peyraut's *Summa virtutum ac viciorum* ('The Complete Book of Virtues and Vices'), or James of Voragine's *Legenda aurea* ('The Golden Legend': a compendium of saints' Lives), and many more, all standard reading for clergy, not to mention some laity, by the time printing arrived to multiply copies still further.

By that date—say, 1450—the best-sellers I have just named would have been joined, and in some regions surpassed, by a manual of moral 'Dos and Don'ts' called the *Praeceptorium,* by the Dominican Johannes Nider. His name betrays him: Nider was a German. This brings me to the one remaining observation we made from our space-satellite: the expansion of Christendom in the north. This expansion had been going on since before the millennium, but its visible effect on Christianity was slower than in the south because it depended on the slow improvement of colonial territory. The process is well described in Robert Bartlett's *The Making of Europe*: it was a bit like America's Wild West, but was a Wild East—a world, not of old Roman cities with their rentier bishops, but of entrepreneurs, lumberjacks, new prairies, and strange people called Slavs. By the fourteenth century, Bohemia, by the fifteenth, Poland, boasted galloping economies. At the same time the Mediterranean of the north—I refer of course to the Baltic and North Sea—had become *mare nostrum* to the cities of the German Hansa, whose position would be challenged only, in the fifteenth century, by the rising states of Holland,

Denmark, and Hohenzollern Prussia, with their state-protected fleets. Of course all this north-eastern development affected urban life in the north-west, too. The most palpable beneficiary was industrial Flanders, whose cheap food (imported from the newly-opened prairies, like our Kellogg's Corn Flakes) and acquisition of new distant markets underlay the flamboyant culture of the duchy of Burgundy—the one described in Huizinga's famous *The Waning of the Middle Ages*.

That was how the northern macrocosm changed. Its effect on the Christian religion had two aspects, of which the first was naturally geography, as the church's centre of gravity moved northwards in sympathy. Around 1300, the *enfant terrible* monarchy in Paris had added a halo to its more earthy recent acquisitions, by getting the late King Louis IX, now *Saint* Louis, canonized. Building on that, Philip IV proceeded publicly to challenge the fundamentals of papal power, money, and jurisdiction, and won. The victory put France on the way to being a prototype modern state. Its magnetic force duly pulled the papacy northwards, to Avignon, from 1316, where the French affinities of the Avignon papacy made it a ghost, this time, not of ancient Caesars but, by anticipation (if you can have ghosts by anticipation), of a national church. It was a faint ghost, but became less faint in 1378, when the Italians reacted and tried to reclaim the papacy for Rome, with the result that the papacy split in two and there were two popes, at Rome and Avignon. (On hearing of the schism, Charles V of France is said to have exclaimed, 'Now I am king and pope.') For twenty-seven years the Great Schism scandalized the world and half-paralysed the church, and its end only brought the image of national churches still nearer. For the council of Constance in 1415, which healed the Schism, was also called to 'reform' the church, a mission its successor at Basle, fifteen years later, sought to continue. But most of the reforms were designed to slim down the papacy, and once the conciliarists had gone home there was no one to enforce the reforms except secular princes. By a judicious use of the red pencil, they sanctioned reforms which strengthened their own churches. That, thought conservative Italians, is what happens when councils meet in Switzerland, not in the Lateran. When the council of Constance deposed the Italian antipope John XXIII, in 1415, a historically-minded German curialist compared the act to Otto the Great's deposition of John XII in 963. Power, in a word, had moved back north.

In 1417 the conciliarists at Constance elected as undisputed pope a Roman of the ancient house of Colonna, Martin V, set him down in Rome, and went home exhausted. Restorations usually disappoint, and this one did. What they had restored was a rump. The Schism had taken away half—the French half—of the papacy's international revenues, and the princely governments were busy removing the other half. The papacy had only its old back garden, the papal states, to live from, and survived by means of an uneasy marriage with their commercial northern neighbour, Florence. We call that marriage the Renaissance. A lot is heard about Renaissance Florence and its great bankers, the Medici, whose banking services to the papacy included the supply of two popes, Leo X and Clement VII. A lot was meant to be heard: rhetoric and civic pride were of the essence of that culture. So we forget the north, and that the Medici were only Europe's second biggest bankers, far behind the Fuggers of Augsburg, whose silver- and gold-mine owning interests stretched far into the colonial north and east. It was Fugger money which, in 1519, the Habsburg Charles V, scourge of the second Medici pope, had to thank for his election as emperor. The contrast with papal finances is striking. Their sources had become mainly local, drawing the popes' political interests with them. Machiavelli could say the papacy had become one Italian state like others—and one almost, we can add, as Machiavellian.

A shift in the Church's geography went with one in its mentality. Let us go back to those mendicant orders. Because the friars had led the way in adapting Catholicism to the life and mentality of towns, they now became its natural ferry to busy northern Europe. Their low-cost spirituality struck root in analogous conditions, as monarchies and municipalities joined forces in slimming down bishoprics. Mendicant spirituality flowed down many channels, most of them hidden far behind the headline events about popes and kings. The lessons to be learned from mendicant sermons, for instance, are far from exhausted, as are those to be learned from and about confession, whose secret kernel was increasingly enwrapped in a pith of perfectly accessible handbooks, on what and how to confess. Or again there are cultural themes. One is Christmas carols. The story of their genesis leads from Franciscan Italy, *via* fourteenth-century Rhineland Dominicans, to Irish and English Franciscans. As for English Franciscans, has anyone ever investigated, seriously, whether one or more of them may have written the Wakefield Mystery Plays, with their striking blend of dramatic force and theological sophistication? Perhaps the broadest spiritual theme inviting study in this connection is that of the real contemplatives of the medieval church, religious women. Men, including friars, were often the Marthas of the equation, always busy. But part of friars' business was to do priestly duties for the women's branch of the order. The effect of preaching, for instance, can work both ways, and it has been plausibly argued that the 'mysticism' for which the Rhineland Dominicans (like Eckhart) became famous was something they had developed through preaching to contemplative women Dominicans.[8] Nor can we explain the ratio of female canonizations in these last two-and-a-half medieval centuries without reference to the mendicants. Some of the famous women, like the Dominican tertiary Catherine of Siena (d. 1380), were actually in mendicant orders, and even the more independent ones enjoyed links with them: like Bridget of Sweden (d. 1397), whose *cause célèbre* canonization was helped on its way by a Dominican biographer.[9]

To suggest that this northern spirituality was entirely the work of mendicants would nevertheless miss the point. For one thing, satire or no satire, not all friars were what they should have been. The orders could themselves become something to be reacted against. But for another, the form of devotion they had pioneered was contagious, with its emphasis on the person of Christ, and on personal simplicity, and its relative flexibility. An important manifestation of urban spirituality was in lay confraternities, some associated, some not, with local friars. In all of them the laity could participate in forms of devotion as pronounced as that to be read in the friars' writings, as can be seen sometimes in church art, for instance in the limewood sculptures of Riemenschneider and Veit Stoss, some of it patronized by confraternities. And some of the spirituality was all but independent of the friars, the best example here being that of the Carthusian order, which, although founded back in 1086, flowered after 1300 and, despite its eremitical way of life, formed a distinct influence in the late medieval church (over 80 per cent of medieval Carthusian foundations and over 90 per cent of their writings come after 1300, and predominantly—as we should expect— north of the Alps).

Connected with the Carthusians, finally, and indirectly with the friars, was the most demonstrably influential of these pre-Reformation spiritual movements, the *Devotio Moderna*, with its offshoot, the 'Brethren of the Common Life'. I say 'indirectly' because this Dutch movement reacted *against* the friars, some of whom replied by trying to suppress it. But no one who has sampled a certain Franciscan tradition of spiritual writing—as in the thirteenth-century novice-master, David of Augsburg— can fail to recognize its tone in that most celebrated production of the *Devotio Moderna*, written around 1426, *The Imitation of Christ*. The tradition I mean can be called that of 'experiential' spirituality, in the sense of matter-of-fact advice by older practitioners of the life of prayer, handed down to youngsters, and based on real-life experience. In this, as in other respects, the *Devotio Moderna* carried all the best genes of medieval spirituality, Cistercian, Carthusian, and mendicant. Likewise, it passed the genes on to Reformation and Post-Reformation Christianity. Not only did the *Imitation* get a prodigious circulation, which still lasts. Calvin, Ignatius, and

Erasmus had all studied in schools run or inspired by the Brethren of the Common Life.

In presenting medieval Christianity to you in terms of material changes, of a kind so big as to be visible from space, I may seem guilty of a kind of dialectical materialism, of wishing to reduce religious experience to a function of economics, and to ignore free will, with its inner response to God—which is what Christianity is all about. But I am not sure the *history* of Christianity is all about that; because these mighty changes that take place about us do, in fact, influence the way we understand our religious duties, even in our prayers, and did then. And because these changes are so large as often to be missed, I see it as a historian's job to discover them and see how they bear on the microcosm, you and me, and the medieval you's and me's who are really our subject.

Another day I might say more about this question, of free will and the array of forces which hedge it about, from stars, or physics, or social circumstance. There was intense interest in the subject in our period, especially (to judge from the literature) in the late thirteenth and fourteenth centuries. But having half-accused myself of forgetting it and then *ex*cused myself, on grounds that it is the mighty changes that are the historian's subject, I would like to end by protesting I have *not* forgotten it, that it was actually there all along. It was there, not just in the everyday lives of the millions of people those vernacular sermons by friars were addressed to—telling them to treat their wives properly, not be crushed by misfortune, not to forget we all have to die sometime; but there also in pious souls who did not have to be told these things but were still sensitive, to the point of pain, of the requirements God made of them. A few of this last category left records: and there, at the very heart of the subject whose outer history I have sketched, is the thing it is all about, the individual will, nestling under God's, and to the utmost degree conscious of doing so.

Two final examples will prove this: one from the eleventh century, from a rural-born southerner, the other from the fifteenth, from a town-born northerner. The first, Anselm of Aosta, came north in the wave of Italian ecclesiastical colonialism that gave half-barbarian Normandy a soul, through its reformed monasteries, and England two archbishops. Anselm was the second of these two archbishops and around 1104 he wrote out the following prayer for his friend, Countess Matilda of Tuscany:

> Almighty God . . .
> May I shun utterly in word and deed,
>   whatever you forbid,
>   and do and keep whatever you command.
> Let me believe and hope, love and live,
>   according to your purpose and will.[10]

The second example is from Thomas à Kempis, whose *Imitation* includes this prayer:

Beloved Father, you are aware of all things; nothing in the conscience of man can escape your notice and you know what is coming before it happens . . . Grant, O Lord, that I may know what I ought to know, and love what I ought to love; that I may praise what most pleases you, value what is precious in your eyes, and reject what you find vile.[11]

Not much change there, that I can see: *no* material for the historian, least of all one looking down from a satellite. If he could look *up* from there, of course . . . But then he would be more than a historian.

6

THE REFORMATION
1500–1650

Diarmaid MacCulloch

The sixteenth-century upheavals in western Latin Christianity represent the greatest fault-line to have appeared in Christian culture since the Latin and Greek halves of the Roman empire went their separate ways a thousand years before. Western society was now torn apart by deep disagreements about how human beings should exercise the power of God in the world, arguments even about what it was to be human.

The division which followed from this between Catholic and Protestant still marks Europe west of the lands of Orthodox Christianity—most obviously for the British in northern Ireland, but everywhere in the continent in a host of attitudes, assumptions, and habits of life which distinguish, for instance, Protestant Prussia from neighbouring Catholic Poland. The decay of actual religious practice in Europe makes it all the more urgent a task to explain the reasons for this continuing diversity. The common Latin inheritance of Catholic and Protestant, besides and beyond their sixteenth-century quarrels, is the shaping fact of European identity, and the inheritance continues to shape Europe's effect on the rest of the modern world. Now for the first time since the Reformation we see the possibility of a unifying institution for our western Latin inheritance in the European Union, and we need to understand what happened then in order to find a sane and informed identity for ourselves in the twenty-first century.

Besides this, the story of the sixteenth-century Reformation is not only relevant to the little continent of Europe. At the same time as the common culture of Latin Christian Europe was falling apart, Europeans established their power in the Americas and on the coasts of Asia and Africa; so all their religious divisions were reproduced there. In the United States of America this diversity achieved a new synthesis; American life is fired by a continuing energy of religious practice derived from the sixteenth century. The Reformation, particularly in its English Protestant form, has created the dominant ideology of the world's one remaining super-power. Reformation ways of thought remain alive in American culture and also in African and Asian Christianity (often alarmingly alive)—this is at a time when they have largely become part of history in their European homeland.

There is much that modern westerners—including modern Christians—are likely to deplore on all sides in the Reformation. Both late medieval Christianity and the mainstream Protestantism which sought to destroy it were religions of fear, anxiety, and guilt, although they also both claimed to produce a remedy and a comfort for anxiety and guilt, through the love exhibited by God to humanity in Jesus Christ. The arguments of the Reformation were in large part about how human beings best approached this love of God, and about whether there was anything in human behaviour and actions which could influence God into saving them from eternal despair. Some of the most interesting answers to these questions came from people who were marginalized and rejected by Catholics and Protestants alike, because they questioned the grim certainties which both sides shared, and suggested that there might be new, more constructive approaches to divine power and its interplay with humanity.

In the past, the Reformation was often seen solely in terms of a handful of significant males, principally Martin Luther, Huldrych Zwingli, John Calvin, Ignatius Loyola, Thomas Cranmer, Henry VIII, and a number of popes. These figures are only part of a story which also involves the movements of popular feeling, the slowly changing lifestyles of ordinary people and the political and dynastic concerns of landed elites. That popular dimension has been one of the rediscoveries of Reformation research over the last century. However, we should not forget that the Reformation was about ideas. One conclusion to be drawn from the accumulation of recent research on the Latin church before the upheaval was that it was not as corrupt and ineffective as Protestants have tended to portray it, and that it generally satisfied the spiritual needs of late medieval people. This is brilliantly expounded for the church in England (admittedly a particularly well-organized part of medieval Europe) in Eamon Duffy's book *The Stripping of the Altars*.[1]

This recovered perspective only serves to emphasize the importance of the ideas which the Reformers put forward. They were not attacking a moribund church which was an easy target, ripe for change, but despite this, their message was still able to seize the imaginations of enough people to overcome the power and success of the old church structures. Ideas mattered profoundly; they had an independent power of their own, and they could be corrosive and destructive. The power of ideas also explains why the Reformation was such a continent-wide event: using the common language of Latin, which all educated people spoke and wrote, religious revolutionaries could spread their message across smaller-scale culture and language barriers. And for that reason, I will unrepentantly concentrate on the thought and effects of a few key thinkers in the Reformation: Luther, Zwingli, Calvin, Loyola.

What becomes clear if one studies the Reformation is that there were a number of crisis points: turning-points when the story could have gone in another direction, but which pulled events decisively on one particular path. Take 1517. That was the year in which the official church's supposedly reforming Lateran Council ended without achieving much, and the same year in which Luther caught the imagination of central Europe as a symbol of social transformation. Another moment was 1525, the culmination of seven years of popular excitement after Luther's challenge, in which anything seemed possible: but it ended in the defeat of the German peasants' rebellion and widespread popular disillusion. Then there were the years 1541–2, a moment when prospects for reunion and civilized settlement of religious arguments were real, only to end in disappointment and futility. After 1541–2, thirty years of indecisive battles followed: then in 1570–2, a series of separate political crises in different parts of Europe shifted the balance in favour of Protestants in the north, and of Catholics in the south. After that, the story of north and south becomes fragmented and moves to different rhythms.

THE OLD CHURCH 1490–1517

The old church was a religious apparatus which very effectively united Europe and contained huge religious diversity within a single structure. Symbols of unity abounded: the Latin language, the administrative organization of the papacy, religious orders with a unified structure, international events like the Frankfurt book fair. The pope could have a say in church affairs from Iceland to Seville, and international orders of friars could sponsor spectacular revivalist devotional movements in the far west of Europe, the Gaelic western shores of Ireland. However, there were strains within the church's structure. One problem for the pope was a political accident: as Alexander Murray has noted in Chapter 5, from the 1490s, he found himself at the crossroads of a war between western Europe's two greatest dynasties, the Habsburg and the Valois. Their struggle for power centred on a struggle for Italy, and that meant that the pope was forced to defend his territories and make alliances like any other Italian prince. He had to behave with as much magnificence as the Habsburg or the Valois. Caught between expenditure on war and on courtly display, his financial resources came under terrible strain. That would be a major part of the accident which was Luther's protest in 1517.

And this military struggle between western Europe's brother-monarchs was all the more painful because the borders of western Christian Europe were under threat from outside: from militant Islam. In the far west, Christianity was winning, pushing back the older wave of Islamic expansion in Spain. There Christianity's triumph was not merely to destroy an Islamic culture, but a Jewish one as well, as the Jews of Spain were scattered throughout the Mediterranean or forced to deny their identity and culture if they stayed. The Christianity of Spain was exceptionally self-confident, intolerant, militant; there was nothing quite like it in the Latin west. But in the east, the Islamic Ottoman empire continued to push in on Europe. In the 1520s it smashed an entire kingdom in Hungary: and in the quarrels of the Reformation, the Latin Christians of central Europe were unable to unite and win back the lost lands. Islam would be a presence in the Adriatic and the former eastern marches of Latin Christianity for the next three centuries. The consequences are with us still in the agonies of the former Yugoslavia.

HOPES AND FEARS 1490–1517

What was important to the Christians of Latin Europe? Naturally, the road to salvation. Out of the varied theological inheritance of the early centuries, western Europe had developed the idea of purgatory, one of the most successful theological concepts in Christian history: a notion which satisfied millions for century after century. It was an effective remedy for the fact that the Christian picture of the afterlife has never been particularly satisfactory. In its earliest form, it consists of two stark alternative fates: heaven and hell, drawn in terms of radical opposites, the greatest bliss versus the greatest misery. The trouble about this picture is that it does not accord with our consciousness of ourselves. For the most part we do not experience ourselves as spectacularly good or spectacularly bad: we are conscious of being imperfect, and want to do a bit better, and that is about it. How does this consciousness of ourselves match up to consignment to eternal bliss or eternal agony? One sensible answer to the problem is to suppose that a merciful God allows us rather more time than our threescore years and ten to do something about our grubby little imperfections: the state of refining and grim hard work in the afterlife, which the medieval Latin church came to know as purgatory.

Purgatory was thus a wonderfully comforting doctrine. It gave human beings a sense that they could do something about their own salvation. They could pray, they could do good works: in fact, their prayer was a good work. They could hire clergy to pray for them, particularly in the highest form of prayer, the Mass, and all this would lessen the time that they had to spend doing good works in the afterlife in order to gain entry to heaven. The whole system became an industry, the purgatory industry: a great factory of prayer and devotional observance. Whatever academic theologians said to qualify the idea, it gave ordinary people the sense that they could work away at sorting out the afterlife. Perhaps it was the people of northern Europe rather than southern Europe who took the doctrine of purgatory particularly to their hearts. Certainly it was northern Europe which came to rebel most bitterly against the idea when questions came.

For there was one big problem with purgatory. Christianity was a religion that claimed that its central truths had been delivered from the mind of God in written form for humans to understand: the Bible. In that collection of writings, it was very difficult to find any reference to purgatory. Creative biblical scholars did, of course, because they always will find something in the Bible if they need to. But mostly it was a case of taking poetic readings of the biblical text, finding images and allegories. That was fine in a world where this was a normal way of reading texts, but in the fifteenth century a new attitude to reading texts emerged: an attitude which has rather clumsily been labelled humanist.

What was humanism? Basic to it was a renewed fascination with the past: ancient Greece and Rome. Western Europeans had repeatedly returned to this past for inspiration; they had done so in the twelfth century, and equally they had done so in the time of Charlemagne, centuries before. But now the effect was more intense than ever before, because there was more to discover about the past. More ancient manuscripts were released into the general scholarly world, partly when modern Greeks brought them west to save them from the invading Ottoman Turks. And these texts could be publicized at vastly greater speed because the west seized on the Chinese idea of printing multiple copies of texts in movable type. The texts revealed previously unsuspected reservoirs of knowledge which could be applied to the present day. They produced the heady feeling that society could be improved and changed by reviving ideas which Europe had forgotten.

But note that all this excitement was based on texts, and to squeeze maximum meaning out of the texts, they had to be read accurately and intensively, gauging what they might have been intended to say in the context of the society which produced them. So a humanist was above all an editor of and commentator on texts. And the central text of all was the Bible. Christian humanists expected to read this greatest gift of God to gain sacred knowledge just as they gained secular knowledge from Greek and Roman literature. Eventually they would begin noticing that purgatory, that central idea for late medieval salvation, did not seem to have been too high on God's agenda when he imparted sacred truth in the biblical record.

And there was an extra spin-off from the humanist fascination with encountering truth in authentic ancient literature. One obvious fact stood out about the western church's sacred text, the Vulgate Bible: it was a translation into Latin from Greek and Hebrew. This had scarcely mattered when very few people even among the finest minds of Latin Europe understood Greek: rather more of them, in fact, understood Hebrew, since there were rather more Jews to argue with in medieval Latin Europe than there were Greeks. However, it was a shock for humanists, and a delightful shock, to encounter the Apostle Paul in the language which he would have spoken. What did that say for the authority of the medieval western church, which had very rarely enjoyed this experience? One of the reasons why the Orthodox churches have never experienced Reformation is that they have never had to face a similar adjustment of authority, having always possessed the text of the New Testament in its original language.

In the short term, however, humanism seemed no threat to the church, more a way of helping it sort out its problems. There was a flood of fresh information on the earliest days of the church, fresh ways of seeing how the church might be viewed. There was a general sense of optimism, even playfulness, and a confidence in new possibilities in church and secular government. These moods were symbolized for instance by the attempts at reform in the 1512–17 Lateran Council in Rome, and by the international reputations and friendships of the humanist Desiderius Erasmus, Thomas More, and Bishop John Fisher. Yet one continuing Christian writer from the distant Roman past still dominated the way that western Christianity approached God: the fifth-century Augustine of Hippo. His theology centred on the tragic contrast between the weakness and imperfection of humanity and the purity and majesty of God. Augustine was a pessimist about the human condition, and he was only an optimist about the possibility that God in his mercy and love might make a free decision to save a part of this worthless, fallen rabble of humanity. Augustine is distinctively the theologian of the Latin western as against the eastern Orthodox churches. The mainstream Protestants were to be as much dominated by Augustine as was the traditional western church. One man in particular became possessed by the same sense of tragedy in humanity which had seized Augustine. He was a German Augustinian monk called Martin Luther.

A NEW HEAVEN AND A NEW EARTH:
1517–1526

Luther's protest was not originally against the big idea of purgatory. In fact, years after he had rebelled against Roman authority, perhaps for a dozen years and more after 1517, he went on believing in purgatory until he saw that it had no place in his scheme of Christian belief. Instead, he seized on lesser problems which many loyal churchpeople had uncontroversially seen as needing reform: details of the medieval scheme of salvation. The particular detail which caused the trouble was the sale of indulgences. Indulgences were grants by the church of remissions of punishment for sin: they could be seen as a demonstration of the love of God for sinners, and a practical demonstration that the love of God was channelled through the power of the church.

However, there were two features of indulgences which aroused Luther's fury: one minor, one major. The minor point was the vulgarity of the idea that such grants could be sold, and sold by authority of the pope himself in a squalid effort to raise funds from the German faithful. Many people besides Luther felt outrage at this, and the fund-raising was particularly squalid in 1517. However, much more fundamental was an idea about salvation which Luther found clashed with his reading of Augustine and of the New Testament. Indulgences were a proclamation that there were powers on earth which could influence the fate of human beings in the afterlife: they were part of the visible church's repertoire of devices for salvation. Indulgences had even come to represent precise mathematical statements about how much time human beings could chop off their stay in purgatory. The notion offended against the majesty of God, and undermined the awful completeness of human sin. Luther had felt his total sinfulness, and he had despaired of ever satisfying God. His answer had been that of Augustine: accept this fact and rely on a gracious gift from God: forgiveness and remission of sins. The work of Christ on the cross had been to proclaim this gift by making the only act of atonement for sin which God could ever accept, because God himself in Christ had performed it. Habakkuk 2: 4 and Romans 1: 17 proclaim that 'the just shall live by faith'—that is, faith in Christ on the cross. It was an exhilarating, liberating idea, because it ended the tyranny of religious observance and of external demands on the human soul. Or that is how it seemed at the time.

So Luther proclaimed a central theme in the writings of Augustine and Paul; but his proclamation was quickly turned into an act of rebellion because the official church gave a heavy-handed and authoritarian response to his protest. That meant that Luther himself was driven to think more radically about the church's faults. He had accepted his total sinfulness: that gave him a paradoxical sense of his own rightness, and if the pope was telling him that he was wrong when he proclaimed God's cause, that must mean that the pope was God's enemy. What was worse, the church had taken God's sacraments and turned them into part of an elaborate confidence-trick on God's people. This passionate conviction made Luther proclaim his message to all the victims of the con-trick: not just to scholars in Latin but to ordinary people in German. He translated the Bible for them, with his own spin on the translation just to make sure that his liberating message got across. He became a symbol of change, and he aroused passionate enthusiasm all through Europe, across different language barriers. It was the most devout people who were aroused by the message that they had been cheated by the church and made to look foolish by their intense round of devotional observances in worship.

But what degree of change was Luther proclaiming, and what needed changing? Many ordinary folk, especially those defending their livelihoods against new demands by their lords and by governments, thought that Luther's defiance of authority was a sign that all authority was collapsing in God's final judgement on human sin. The last days had arrived, and it was the duty of everyone to hurry along God's plan, and help overthrow God's enemies in high places. In 1525 all central Europe was convulsed by revolts against princes and church leaders. The revolts were brutally crushed, and Luther, terrified by the disorder, applauded the rulers' brutality. Another text from Paul's epistle to the Romans lit up for him: (13: 1) 'Let everyone obey the superior powers, for there is no authority except from God'. This has been described as the most important text of the Reformation. Many humanist scholars now drew back from Reformation in fright; others committed themselves to an ordered, systematic, modulated programme of change. That was all the more necessary because for many of the cowed, resentful rebels of Europe, the work of the Reformers now seemed a sham and a betrayal. A widespread sense of disillusion and cynicism confronted the efforts of Luther and his supporters to spread the message of liberation. They would have to find some means for pursuing their revolution.

WOOING THE MAGISTRATE, 1526–1540

What they did was to woo the magistrates—that is, Europe's secular leaders. The leaders of the church, the bishops, were for the most part on the defensive and would not defect from the old organization, but secular rulers might well be interested in a reformation which stressed theologies of obedience and good order and also offered the chance to put the church's wealth to new purposes. In Zürich in Switzerland, another reformer called Huldrych Zwingli had already pioneered a very close union between church and magistrate, in order to promote an idea of reform with the same basis as Luther's. From the early 1520s, Zwingli's church was in effect the city of Zürich, and the magistrates of Zürich could hold debates to decide the nature of the eucharist, just as they were able to make directions for navigation on Lake Zürich or make arrangements for sewage disposal. Luther also now found that he was reliant on German princes for help in two directions: first against ordinary people who did not want to be reformed, and second, against the Holy Roman Emperor Charles V who wished to destroy him and his whole programme of change. In fact, out of this support of the princes came a label for the new movement, when some of the princes supporting Luther made a protest against the decisions of the majority in the Imperial Diet or Assembly in 1529. They were nicknamed Protestants. The nickname stuck.

So the period after 1525 was one in which the traumatic memory of the peasants' rebellion ended any chance of a united continent-wide popular revolution. The magisterial Reformation was created: the Protestant movement led by the *magistri*, the theologically educated masters, and by the magistrates of all descriptions: kings, princes, city councils. There were still many radicals, however, who proposed their own do-it-yourself solutions to Reformation. In Switzerland some were inspired by the fact that Zürich's religious leader Zwingli was much more systematic and logical in his rejection of the past than Luther. They took up Zwingli's thinking on the sacraments of eucharist and baptism: Zwingli rejected the idea that the sacraments had power to bring salvation, and he stressed that they were pledges of faith by Christian believers who had received God's gift of saving faith already. In Zwingli's theology, sacraments were primarily something that Christians did for God, rather than God for Christians. For some enthusiasts, this meant that Christian baptism ought to be a conscious act of faith by the person baptized. Clearly babies could not make such an act of faith, so baptism ought to be reserved for adults. Infant baptism was worthless, and so those who consciously sought true baptism should be given a new and genuine baptism. Hence these radicals were called by their enemies (not by themselves) rebaptizers: Anabaptists.

Zwingli was appalled at this logical deduction from his own theology, because it contradicted another axiom of his thought, that the church of Zürich consisted of the whole city of Zürich. If you opted in to baptism, making a positive decision for it as an adult, you split the wholeness of the community into believers and non-believers. That would end the assumption which both he and Luther held as dear as the pope, that all society should be part of the church. So Zürich persecuted Anabaptists, drowning them in the local river, just at the time when the old church began persecuting champions of the magisterial Reformation. The Anabaptists were harried out of ordinary society. They therefore began stressing their difference from ordinary society. When they turned to the Bible for guidance, just as Luther had done, they noticed quite correctly that early Christians had separated themselves from ordinary society, if such books of the Bible as the book of Acts were to be believed. Acts talked of Christians holding all goods in common. 'Do not swear at all' said Jesus Christ as recorded by the evangelist Matthew (5: 34). 'Commit no murder' said the Ten Commandments. So Anabaptists created their own little worlds, in which goods were held in common, where no one would swear the oaths which governments demanded, or take up the sword when rulers ordered them to. It was infuriating and terrifying for rulers who expected the obedience due in Romans 13: 1.

More frightening still was that some radicals continued to believe that their new societies were destined to usher in the last days by force. They heard Matthew's Jesus say, 'I have come not to send peace, but a sword' (Matt. 10: 34), and they wanted to help God fulfil his political programme in the book of Revelation. So within a decade of central Europe's convulsions in the 1525 peasants' revolt, groups from the Low Countries in the extreme west began joining with other radicals in converging on the German city of Münster. They arrived in their thousands; they took over, and their charismatic leaders proclaimed the new Jerusalem in Münster. A joint force of Lutherans and Catholics besieged them. Under pressure, with their city beginning to starve, the radicals' revolution turned to nightmare; they became the Khmer Rouge of the sixteenth century; Münster entered Year Zero.

Their Pol Pot was a young Dutchman, Jan Beuckelszoon, or John of Leyden, who lived as their king in insane luxury, surrounded by his harem, as his followers starved and died defending him. In the end Münster Anabaptists were sadistically suppressed by the besieging armies. Radicalism turned from militancy, to quiet, non-militant escapes from ordinary society. Yet Münster remained in the minds of the frightened rulers of Europe as a constant enduring nightmare: peaceable, inoffensive Anabaptists were burned and harried because of the memory of John of Leyden.

The challenge of radicalism to Western Christianity was in fact more long-term and subtle than this. Some radicals questioned the assumption that Christianity ought to have an alliance with the powerful: that was an assumption which had been general for a thousand years before, since the time of Constantine the Great. Some questioned as to whether there should be one church at all, or that there should be any coercion of beliefs, or that there was any one normative perception of truth. Others looked at the Bible, and could not find the doctrines which the church said were there, in particular the Trinity. Some continued to find in its pages a doctrine which the church said was definitely not there: exclusively adult baptism. Some came to the conviction that the Bible was not the ultimate guide to divine truth, and that God spoke to the individual as he (or even she) pleased. In the end, it may be the radicals in the Reformation who can claim the victory, for all these notions can now be found in the churches which are the heirs of the magisterial Reformation, even within the church of Rome which opposed it.

Yet the magisterial reformers went on battling for the

minds of rulers. They failed in the case of France and of the Habsburgs: they succeeded in much of Germany and Scandinavia. They gained a curious sort of victory in England, where the murderously opinionated monarch Henry VIII found an alliance with the Reformation useful in the course of his eccentric marital adventures. With the quiet encouragement of his great minister Thomas Cromwell and Archbishop Thomas Cranmer, Henry gradually let slip more and more of the old devotional system. In Slav central Europe, Lutheranism appeared to be gaining the upper hand against the traditional church, especially because the chaos in the ruins of the kingdom of Hungary left a situation wide open for many varieties of religious reform, and individual noblemen took up the cause of reform in different ways. The most interesting and apparently one of the most successful solutions to the relationship of church and state in the period was the Reformation of Strasbourg, led by a former Dominican friar, Martin Bucer. Strasbourg looked like the centre of the future Reformation, for Bucer was a self-proclaimed (if fatally verbose) broker of consensus amid the Reformers' disagreements, and the city was at the heart of European trade and culture. In fact, Strasbourg was to fall away from European leadership because of military defeat, and then there would be other contenders.

REUNION DEFERRED: 1540–1553

First, however, was a moment of general hope, in 1541–2. In these years, prospects for reunion and a civilized settlement of religious arguments were high, though they were mostly to end in disappointment and futility. Open-minded humanist leaders in the Roman church sought to find agreement with the rebel reformers, but even though they had the warm backing of the Holy Roman Emperor, they failed to clinch an ambitious scheme of reconciliation proposed in discussions at Ratisbon (Regensburg). After that, hardliners were heard more loudly in Rome, and some key southern European Catholic reformers fled north in panic to seek refuge with Protestants. A prince-bishop in Germany, Hermann von Wied, failed to lead a Reformation in Cologne which had involved Martin Bucer, and which would have been an example to other bishops of how to find a middle path of change within the old structures. The time for humanist moderation was past. A council of the Roman church began meeting in 1545 at Trent, in a mood of triumphalist aggression. Now there were signs that the old church would find its own dynamism and regain its self-confidence.

At the heart of this new mood was the Society of Jesus. It was fired with the enthusiasm of militant Spanish religion, led by an ex-soldier from the Basque country, Ignatius Loyola. Like Luther, Ignatius had a crisis of faith, but his crisis led in the opposite direction to Luther's: not rebellion against the church, but a soldier's obedience to God's lieutenant on earth, the pope. His first thought was to fight for Christianity in the Holy Land. When that idea failed to get off the ground, his plan became to battle for a renewal of spiritual fervour among loyal children of the church like himself. Only gradually did the Jesuits stumble on a mission to wage spiritual warfare on Protestantism; but by the late 1540s, it looked as if politics was on their side at last. The Holy Roman Emperor confronted his Protestant princes and smashed them in 1547; he also ended the independent career of the Reformation in Strasbourg. Momentarily, it looked as if England would take over the leadership of the magisterial Reformation, in the reign of Henry VIII's boy-king son, Edward VI, but this hope was dashed when Edward died in 1553 and the kingdom dramatically rejected his chosen successor Queen Jane Grey in favour of the Catholic Lady Mary. Luther was dead by 1546, Zwingli long-dead. The hopes for the triumphal assertion of God's word expressed in the Bible seemed doomed. The last days had not arrived. Many had rejected the message. What could be done?

The person who led Protestantism out of stagnation in the 1550s was an exiled Frenchman who had wandered Europe and ended up by accident in Geneva. His name was John Calvin. He probably never liked Geneva very much, but he felt that God had sent him there for a purpose, and so he resigned himself to a dour struggle to stay there and lead God's work in the city. After one false start, he was thrown out of Geneva, but that gave him the chance to go to Strasbourg and see how a Reformation might be put into practice. When the Genevans faced chaos and called him back in desperation, Calvin was ready to build a better Strasbourg in Geneva. It took him years to secure the task, but the Genevans never dared lose face by throwing him out a second time, and in the end one event which we might regard as tragic made his name on a European-wide scale. In 1553 he was faced with the arrival in Geneva of a prominent radical intellectual, an exile like himself, a Spaniard called Michael Servetus. Servetus denied that the church's conventional notion of the Trinity could be found in the Bible; he had already been condemned by the pope's Inquisition as a heretic. Calvin saw his duty as clear: Servetus must die. So the city authorities burned Servetus at the stake, though Calvin wanted a more merciful death like beheading. Thus Calvin established that the Protestants meant business just as much as Catholics in representing mainstream traditional Christianity.

Consistently with this, Calvin wrote and repeatedly rewrote a textbook of doctrine which he called the *Institution of the Christian Religion*: commonly known as the *Institutes*. This was designed to lay claim to Catholic Christianity for the Reformation: since the pope opposed the Reformation, he was Antichrist, and the Protestants were the true Catholics. Calvin could explain the failures of the Reformation by reference to a doctrine which Luther had also held, but had not emphasized: God's plan of predestination. If salvation was entirely in the hands of God, as Luther said, and human works were of no avail, then logically God would take a decision on individual salvation without reference to the life-story of an individual. He would decide to save some, and logically also he would also decide to damn others. His scheme of predestination would thus be double. Evidently those who did not listen to and act on the Word were among the damned: and that lessened the sense of disappointment that not all heeded the Reformation message. The good news was that the elect of God could not lose their salvation. The doctrine of election became ever more important, and ever more comforting and empowering, to Calvin's followers.

Consciously Calvin sought the middle ground among the

reformers. He was saddened by the division between the Swiss and the Lutheran loyalists about just what the eucharist meant, and he proposed his own solution to the problem, based on the groundwork laid by Martin Bucer in Strasbourg. He satisfied most of the Swiss, but not the German ayatollahs fiercely guarding Luther's theological legacy: they stuck as strongly as the pope himself to the idea that the flesh and blood of Christ were present in the bread and wine of the eucharist. As a result, Calvin's attempt to unite Protestantism against the Roman menace ironically resulted in a deeper divide among Protestants. Lutheran loyalists increasingly directed the Protestantism of northern Europe, northern Germany and Scandinavia. Elsewhere, the powerful prose and driving intellectual energy of Calvin's *Institutes* inspired a whole variety of churches who felt that Luther had not gone far enough. Other major theologians lined up with Calvin against hardline Lutheranism, often with regret at the division, but seeing little other option: such figures as the exiled Polish bishop Jan Łaski, the one-time star preacher of Italy Peter Martyr Vermigli, the charismatic wandering Scot John Knox. More cautiously, the older established Protestant churches of Switzerland made common cause with Calvin. Together all these communities created a second Protestant identity besides Lutheranism: the Reformed. Reformed Christianity was the movement which saved the Reformation from its mid-century phase of hesitation and disappointment. Lutheranism remained frozen in German-speaking and Scandinavian cultures. Reformed Christianity spread through a remarkable variety of language-groups and communities.

Wars of Religion: 1553–1570

In particular, Calvinism showed a new militancy and a rebellious spirit in the service of the magisterial Reformation. Calvin had taken much inspiration from Luther, and like Luther, he was a theologian of Romans 13: 1: of obedience. Yet as he built his church in Geneva, he was much more careful than Luther to keep the church's structure separate from the existing city authorities in Geneva. He had a clear vision of God's people making decisions for themselves: his church had a mind of its own over against the secular power, just as much as the old church of the pope. In Geneva this was not a problem, after Calvin had clawed his way to political dominance, because church and state were in general agreement, but elsewhere, people might take up Calvin's blueprint for church structures and ignore what the state desired or ordered. To Calvin's alarm, he found that he had sponsored a movement of militant revolution, people inspired by the thought that they were the elect army of God against Antichrist.

Very often the revolutionary Reformed leaders were actually noblemen rebelling against their monarchs, rather than the humble enthusiasts of the Anabaptists, and that made their rebellion all the more effective. Noblemen could harness traditional loyalties as well as the destructive enthusiasm of mobs who wanted to smash the old church physically: great crowds determined to fight Antichrist broke stained glass windows and hurled down statues, roaring out the Psalms of David in easy-to-remember rhymes set to popular song-tunes. The effect was startling. In Calvin's lifetime, Reformed Protestant Frenchmen began challenging the French monarchy, and it took fifty years of warfare and royal treachery for the monarchy to bring them to heel. Other Reformed activists humiliated and then dethroned the Catholic Queen of Scots: they threw off Catholic Spanish rule in the northern Netherlands, they terrified and bewildered the Turks in eastern Europe by their militancy. The church in England was deeply affected by their style of piety, despite the hostility of a Protestant monarch, Queen Elizabeth, who was nearly as self-willed in her theological outlook as her father King Henry.

The result by 1570 was a Europe in which the divisions were increasingly clear. A series of separate political crises in different parts of Europe around 1570 shifted the balance in favour of Protestants in the north and in favour of Catholics in the south. People were forced to make decisions, or at least their rulers forced decisions on them. Which checklist of doctrine did they sign up to? The Augsburg Confession and the Formula of Concord of the Lutherans? The Heidelberg Catechism and the other confessions of the Reformed? The Decrees of the Council of Trent? Historians have given an unlovely but perhaps necessary jargon label to this process: 'confessionalization'—that is, the creation of fixed identities and systems of beliefs for separate churches which had previously been more fluid in their self-understanding, and which had not sought separate identities for themselves.[2] Confessionalization represents the defeat of attempts to rebuild the unified Latin church.

The contrasting stories in north and south after 1570 can be symbolized by the fortunes of two navies of the Spanish empire: one was victorious, the other was destroyed. A

Spanish Mediterranean fleet crushingly defeated the Turkish fleet at Lepanto in 1571: that was one of the most decisive checks on Islamic expansion into Western Europe. Far to the north, the other Spanish Armada was outmanoeuvred in the English Channel by Queen Elizabeth's naval commanders in 1588, and it was scattered by the storms of the North Sea and the Atlantic, never to achieve a Roman Catholic conquest of Protestant England. The problem for the future was the exact boundary between these two halves of Europe, since the power of the Catholic Habsburgs straddled north and south. The problem was made worse because in the mid-century struggles, an eventual truce in 1555 between Catholics and Protestants had reflected the realities of that time: the bulk of Protestants fighting the Catholics had been Lutherans. By the end of the century the third force, the Reformed grouping, had emerged, often on the basis of conversion from Lutheranism. The Reformed had no place in the 1555 agreement. This instability was the background to the eventual outbreak of continent-wide war in 1618. Only after thirty years did an exhausted and ravaged Europe establish a religious frontier which largely endures to the present day.

In southern Europe, the renewed dynamism of the old church was in alliance with the various rulers of the Habsburg dynasty: a force which has often been termed the Counter-Reformation—perhaps better, the Catholic Reformation. By the end of the century the Spanish Habsburg monarchy had become the first world power, with a presence in every continent except Australasia. This led to the first large-scale effort to export Latin Christianity to the rest of the world, through Catholic missionary work in America, Asia, and

Africa. The work was done at a time when Protestants were still struggling over their identities, and undertook little missionary outreach beyond their own territories. The Catholic religious orders, and the new variant on the regular religious life, the Society of Jesus, led the Roman church's effort of mission, and particularly in the Far East, they took this mission beyond the military might of the Spanish empire. Here the missionaries had to present Christianity without the backing of coercion, to people of ancient and equally sophisticated faith who might question what good this European export was to them. So it was the Church of Rome which was faced for the first time with the questions which now affect all worldwide Christian attempts at expansion: what is Christian about Christianity? How much of it is a reflection of particular attitudes formed at particular times? How does the message of its sacred books transfer to cultures with other sacred books? Such questions convulsed the first European Christian missions in Asia, and different missionaries came up with different answers. To begin with, the more conservative answers gained the approval of the authorities, and the mission was correspondingly hamstrung. The questions did not go away.

So by the early seventeenth century, Europe had become a deeply divided society. The division was not merely twofold between Roman Catholic and Protestant, but also between Lutheran and Reformed. The Church of England was a puzzle as well: was it part of the Reformed world, or as a minority among its members maintained, something distinctive and closer to the sacramentalist Catholicism of the old church? This clash of identities in the English church was one of the major reasons why a Civil War broke out in the British Isles in 1642: it was a Civil War in which Protestants fought Protestants to decide the future shape of British religion. In the short term the admirers of John Calvin won; they carried Calvinist theologies of resistance to the ultimate when they cut off the head of King Charles I in 1649. In the end they were defeated and thrust aside because their regime was too tidy and too straitlaced for the people of England, and because they could find no popular substitute for the monarchy. The Commonwealth and Oliver Cromwell abolished Christmas and tore down maypoles. The English people refused to open their shops on Christmas Day, and in the end they summoned back both the maypoles and King Charles II. The Church of England which Charles restored was much more obviously out of step with the Reformed ethos than it had been before the war. So in the twenty-year civil wars of the British Isles, a new identity was born for the Church of England, which has since been labelled Anglicanism: a religious outlook which has kept its distance from the rest of the Reformation but also from Rome, and is prepared to live with the ambiguous consequences.

The divisions of Europe would be readily apparent to anyone visiting it in 1600. The passage of time itself was different in different parts of the continent. Protestant societies which had rejected the power of the saints developed a new pattern of the year, in which there were no saints' days; so holidays ceased to be the holy days of the saints and were reinvented as Protestant feasts. In England, yearly bonfires and celebrations reminded the English of their Protestant heritage in defeating the Armada and foiling a

Roman Catholic who had tried to blow up the King and Parliament. By contrast, the Europe which was loyal to Rome discovered new saints and new festivals to emphasize the loyalty. The worship in Roman Catholic churches became ever more splendid and expressive of the power and magnificence of the Church of God, as a backdrop to this world of feast and fast. When Pope Gregory XIII reformed the entire calendar of the year, from 15 October 1582, Protestants took this overdue scientific correction as a sinister papist plot and ignored it—so Europe's clocks and calendars were now divided indeed. But having made the right decision over the calendar, Rome made a disastrous scientific miscalculation in the affair of Galileo Galilei. The Roman authorities forced him to deny his own observations that the earth moved round the sun and not the other way round, because the observations challenged the authority of the church as the source of knowledge.

Yet it should be noted that Protestant churches were as suspicious of the new science of observation as Catholics. For there was much to unite the Church of Rome and the magisterial Reformations. Both based their Christianity on the pronouncements of the Bible, however much they disagreed on what the Bible meant. Those who appeared to challenge that ultimate authority, like radical Christians or Galileo, could find themselves regarded as enemies of God. Similarly, on both sides of the Reformation, Europe became a newly intensively regulated society, as Catholics and Protestants vied with each other to show just how moral a society they could create. Erasmus had given European monarchs the text with his rhetorical question 'What else is the state but a great monastery?'[3] It was a call to rulers to assert their power in people's lives, and to churchmen to give them every assistance. When Protestants closed the old monasteries *en masse*, Erasmus's question became all the more pressing. Both sides shut down the brothels which the medieval church had licensed as a safety-valve for society; both sides stepped up the pressures to suppress male homosexuality. Both sides, with the honourable exceptions of Martin Luther and the Spanish Inquisition (a surprising combination), encouraged the persecution of people who were thought to be witches, that is the agents of the Devil. The Reformation era was the first period in which convicted witches had been executed in great numbers. Both sides remained suspicious and contemptuous of other religions, although Protestants were more inclined to tolerate Jews because they found Jewish biblical scholarship a useful tool against Catholics.

Few people in modern European society now understand just how urgent the arguments of the Reformation were to the people of the sixteenth century. We must see why Europeans were prepared to burn and torture each other because they disagreed on whether, or how, bread and wine were transformed into God, or about the sense in which Jesus Christ could be both divine and human. In exploring these questions, we must not adopt an attitude of intellectual or emotional superiority, especially in the light of the atrocities which twentieth-century Europe has produced because of its faith in newer, secular ideologies. Anxiety and a sense of imperfection seem to be basic components of being human, for the non-religious as well as the religious. The answers of the past to these human agonies may not seem like sensible answers now, but they deserve our respect and an attempt at comprehension. If we cannot understand what made the Reformation work, then we may not be able to tackle a further question. Why, uniquely among world cultures, have the descendants of Latin Christianity begun to emancipate themselves from the bonds of traditional belief-systems? How did the Enlightenment emerge from the spiritual agonies of Martin Luther and his brooding on the legacy of Augustine of Hippo? But that is a question which I am spared from answering. It can be reserved for a later chapter.

7

THE LATE SEVENTEENTH AND EIGHTEENTH CENTURIES

Jane Shaw

In his 1984 BBC series and accompanying book, *The Sea of Faith*, the Cambridge theologian Don Cupitt aimed to show the effects on Christian doctrine of 'the slow process of secularisation, the impact of science and then of biblical and historical criticism, the shift to an ever more man-centred outlook, the encounter with other faiths, and then finally the awesome and still incomplete transition into modernity'. He located the origins of these intellectual and social movements in the eighteenth century, in the age of Enlightenment. Cupitt judged the impact of Enlightenment critical thinking on 'the supernatural dogmatic beliefs of Christianity' to be 'very severe' and stated that 'theologians have been attempting ever since to pick up the pieces with—on their own admission—only limited results'. So for Cupitt, heir of the Enlightenment *par excellence*, how we got to where we are now is quite simple: the critical thinkers of the Enlightenment enabled us to break away from the superstitions of a former age, so that now, when thinking about medieval and early modern notions of God's power, for example, 'we cannot help recognising infantile fantasies of omnipotence for what they are'.[1] Liberated by the Enlightenment, confident of our own progress, we can move on to believing in the sort of non-realist God which Cupitt has in mind.

It is possible that some or even many of you here today, having come to hear a lecture about the history of Christianity in the late seventeenth and eighteenth centuries, in a series on 'how we got to where we are now', will be expecting me to engage in a discussion of the Scientific Revolution, the scepticism of the French *philosophes*, statistics of declining church attendance and the radical atheist politics of at least some participants in the French Revolution, with the intention of arriving at a conclusion not unlike that of Don Cupitt, if by a more historically nuanced route. And yet, in the last two or three decades, historical scholarship on this period has shifted our understanding of that movement we call 'the Enlightenment' enormously. Historians of science, medicine, gender, race, ideas, society, and culture, as well as politics and religion, still see the eighteenth century as a vital turning point—that moment when the West shifts gears and enters modernity—but they also suggest that the story is not quite as simple as we once thought, nor is it all sweetness and light. There were many undersides to that movement we know as the Enlightenment, as illustrated by the newer scholarship which takes into account a broader field of actors—the ordinary people as well as the social elites, Africans as well as white Europeans, women as well as men, those engaged in religious practice rather than the writing of philosophy.

It is my hope to give you some taste of this new scholarship on the Enlightenment by indicating and illustrating some of the ways it has made us think differently about the history of Christianity in the late seventeenth and eighteenth centuries, and thus about the Enlightenment's impact on Christianity today. In particular I want to do this by focusing on England in relation to the rest of Europe and the wider world, and on America—for reasons which I *hope* will become apparent.

The model of the Enlightenment which has tended to prevail has really been based on the way things happened in France—the very term 'Enlightenment' is generally associated with France and with the work of the *philosophes*, men like Voltaire, Diderot, and Montesquieu, whose ideas represented an elite, sceptical outlook on the world. For them, rational man was at the centre of the universe. Some of them saw the universe as a clockwork cosmos created by the divine watch-maker, while others of them understood it to be entirely material, spontaneously generated of eternal matter, a universe in which a figure called God had no part. For many of these philosophers, Christian liturgy was merely mumbo-jumbo, the church an oppressive institution. As Voltaire wrote, 'The institution of religion exists only to keep mankind in order, and to make men merit the goodness of God by their virtue. Everything in a religion which does not tend towards this goal must be considered alien or dangerous.'

Many of the French *philosophes*, but especially Voltaire,

championed religious toleration, in the sense that they exposed to ridicule any form of religious bigotry. But this was really a desire for toleration of free-thinking and any rational form of religion of which they approved: they were quick to condemn any form of Christianity which they considered irrational, most particularly Roman Catholicism. Their context goes some way to explaining their attitudes: the Reformation debates had provoked long and bitter bloodshed in many parts of Europe, as Professor MacCulloch relates, and the absolutist Roman Catholicism of the French king had meant that religion in France took a particularly authoritarian turn, not least when Louis XIV revoked the Edict of Nantes in 1685, an edict which had given toleration to the Huguenots, the French Protestants.

We can, then, find a model of the Enlightenment such as Don Cupitt outlines: it occurs in the salons of eighteenth-century France and in the writings of the *philosophes*, that is, amongst an educated French elite. However, while the French model—of antagonism between new scientific and philosophical ideas and old and out-of-date religion—works for France, it is not the template by which we should understand attitudes towards Christianity in this period in the rest of Europe or further afield, even though for many years historians led us to believe it was.

By way of comparison and to suggest a different model of 'Enlightenment', let's turn to England, for it is now generally agreed that the movement called 'the Enlightenment' occurred first in England and it is related to that intellectual impulse we often call the 'Scientific Revolution', to the work of philosophers like Locke, and to the free discussion and demonstration of ideas in the newly emerging public sphere. Yes, we might well point to Descartes' rational philosophy—'I think, therefore I am'—as foundational of so much in Enlightenment thought, but there is a case to be made for his incorporation into English philosophy and culture alongside or even before his work caught on in his native France.

During the sometimes difficult days of the Civil War and the Commonwealth, the 1640s and 1650s, groups of scholars in Oxford, Cambridge, and elsewhere responded to philosophical developments and gathered to discuss them. In Cambridge, it was the translation of Descartes into English which caused keen philosophical debate. In Oxford, it was mechanical natural philosophy which prevailed: Robert Boyle and Robert Hooke invented the air pump, a paradigmatic piece of equipment which was needed for the new experiments and which was therefore central to the methods which could produce 'factual' scientific knowledge. But such knowledge was not just the product of individual practitioners and thinkers, as is sometimes suggested by the ways in which the story of the Scientific Revolution is told; rather it was public knowledge, debated, discussed, and demonstrated among all those who expressed an interest. I imagine Boyle might well have demonstrated his air pump in the Queen's Lane, Oxford coffee house (founded in 1654) on many an occasion. If you want to get a glimpse of that world, the interconnections between science, religion, and philosophy, and the ways in which the scientific method was beginning to be invented and applied, then read Iain Pears' 1997 brilliant and imaginative novel, *An Instance of the Fingerpost*, which is set in 1650s Oxford.

Late seventeenth-century England witnessed the emergence

of the public sphere—the free and public discussion of ideas which, I suspect, every single one of us here takes for granted. The emergence of this public sphere occurred through the development of new media: cheap print culture, coffee houses, public gardens, lending libraries, and institutions such as the Royal Society—a society given its Royal Charter in 1662, which grew out of those groups of scholars meeting at the universities in the 1650s. The Royal Society stood at the heart of a network of European and American scholars who, through the Society's published *Transactions*, could discuss their ideas and experiments with one another. These various new media expanded the traditional means of communication and debate—the pulpit and the public house. They could have developed anywhere, given the right political climate, but it was England, gasping for air after the chaos of the Civil War, which created the environment for them initially.

Furthermore the public sphere emerged first in England, too, because of the ways in which the English had to grapple with the problems of religion, toleration, and politics. After the heavy emotional and political toll of the Civil War period, in which numerous new Protestant sects had sprung up, each claiming their own authority, a desire for religious toleration and peace prevailed, as John Locke's writings about toleration illustrate. Furthermore, the Roman Catholicism of Charles II and, more acutely, of James II provoked fears of absolutism like that being exercised by Louis XIV across the water. In effecting the so-called 'Glorious Revolution' in which the Protestant William of Orange from the Netherlands and his English wife Mary were put on the throne without bloodshed, English leaders paved the way for a constitutional settlement which balanced the trinity of monarch, parliament, and established church and secured freedom of speech and toleration of religion—albeit a limited religious toleration. These were all things hoped for by many of the *philosophes* in eighteenth-century France: England had got there first, and also produced the philosophers who would influence and shape French Enlightenment thought. The French *philosophes* found themselves returning again and again to agree or debate with Locke's idea that all knowledge is based on observation and experience, or to draw on the work of radical English deists, men like John Toland, when attacking the sanctity of the church or corrupt Christianity.

Current historical thinking therefore points to the occurrence of an early Enlightenment in England, one emerging out of and engaged with religious debates and ideas. Science and religion were not opposed: the Royal Society counted many clergymen amongst its members, and most of its members would have subscribed to the idea that a reading of the Book of Nature could contribute to religious truth and ensure right religious belief and practice. The English Enlightenment was also, perhaps, a more domestic affair, engaged with ordinary people and their religious practices. Let me illustrate these various points by way of a story.

On the evening of 26 November 1693, a thirteen-year-old lame girl named Marie Maillard who lived in London was instantly healed while reading the Bible. It was a day when she had been especially reminded of her lameness because local boys had teased her and thrown dirt at her as she had been walking home. She had just eaten supper and was reading the second chapter of Mark, 'where is related the cure of the man sick of the palsy', when her thigh bone snapped 'just as the words were out of my mouth, and I said, Madam, I am cured'. She ran about and showed her perfectly upright body and now even hips to Madame Laulan, the French gentlewoman with whom she lived. Maillard was a Huguenot who had escaped with her family to London in 1689 from persecution in France. She had been lame since birth because of a tumour which had caused her to tip to one side when she walked. Eminent Huguenot surgeons had pronounced her incurable.

This is a fascinating story, suggesting the ways in which Protestants, a century and a half after the Reformation, had come to accept the possibility of miracles, having once cast them aside as nastily 'papist'. Indeed, we might call this a perfectly Protestant miracle, occurring as it did through the reading of the Bible and thus without the presence of any suspicious intermediary figures. As word spread of Maillard's cure, she inspired at least three other women living in London, two Baptists and one Anglican, to read the Bible in hope of a miraculous cure, and indeed all three declared themselves miraculously healed of apparently hopeless cases of, respectively, the palsy, lameness, and an unpleasant skin disease.

However, if we look at the wider responses to Maillard's cure, we find a set of events which reveals to us much about the relationship between science and religion, medicine and politics, at the end of the seventeenth century in England. For Maillard did not only inspire copycat cases amongst other Protestant women of the lower orders, she also attracted the attention of the Queen, at least three prominent Church of England bishops, the Lord Mayor of London, and various doctors, including one James Wellwood, a Fellow of the Royal

College of Surgeons, whose comments on the case suggest to us something about the relationship between science and religion in the early days of the English Enlightenment. Wellwood declared that he was 'not ashamed to own, that there is something in it [the cure] which I cannot well comprehend, and shall not be angry with anybody that ascribe to it something above or out of the Road of Nature'. Indeed he admitted to the mystery of both science and religion. 'If it is said, why should God work such a Miracle, if it be any? (as I shall never determine) I must own . . . that if I do not know all the secrets of Nature, I do much less know the secrets of the Author of Nature.'[2] The bishops who became interested in the case agreed: miracles remained plausible, but the new science made it clear that full and proper evidence was always required. Hence those who were interested in Maillard's case examined her healed body and collected large numbers of affidavits from all those who had know her before and after the cure. Proper evidence for the miracle was vital but if, by that evidence, the miracle were 'proven' true but still denied, then the dangers of scepticism and irreligion were invited— and these were just as threatening as the 'enthusiasm' and 'superstition' (to use the language of the day) of those who believed any religious phenomenon too readily and on their own authority. If, for most of us, our 'touchstone' for attitudes to miracles in the eighteenth century is David Hume's utterly sceptical approach (*Of Miracles*, 1748) we should remember that Hume's contribution came at the end of a long debate on miracles, was not typical of the majority of positions in that debate, and exactly epitomized the 'irreligious' stance which the majority of 'reasonable' Anglicans and nonconformists feared. We should not be surprised that bishops and medical doctors took the line they did in response to Maillard's case. Their approach is typical of that taken by many members of the Royal Society in the late seventeenth century and the eighteenth century who wanted to synthesize the New Philosophy and the central tenets of Christianity, and to take the methods of science and apply them to 'test' any contentious phenomena (such as miracles). Their task was to steer a middle course between the private, emotional religion of enthusiastic Protestants, who relied too much on their own authority, and the scepticism of more radical philosophers like the deists (about whom I shall have more to say later) whose freethinking was perceived to be a threat to the established church. If there was an Anglican Enlightenment it was this: faith had to stand up to public, rational, and scientific scrutiny.[3]

It is exactly this approach we see at play in much of the current work on religion and science: I am thinking here, for example, of the Templeton Foundation's ongoing study of the effects of prayer in an American hospital, where 1200 heart-surgery patients are being used as the bodies of evidence, as described in Russell Stannard's recent book, *The God Experiment*.[4] Some of the patients are being prayed for and know it; some are being prayed for and don't know it; and some are not being prayed for—at least not by the special prayer team. The experiment is interesting, for our purposes, for the ways in which it embodies in its methods the prevailing attitudes of Enlightenment England towards the relationship between religion and science. The nineteenth and twentieth centuries may have seen a deep split between science and religion in many quarters but scholars working in the field of science and religion *now* seem to be returning to a synthesis of the two disciplines which scholars of the late seventeenth and eighteenth centuries necessarily assumed.

Let me turn now to spirituality and religious practice, for Marie Maillard's Bible reading in this story raises the issue of the practice of piety. The eighteenth century has not been seen as a particularly pious time. When, in the 1980s, I was planning my doctoral research on eighteenth-century English Christianity many people expressed surprise: what was there to write about religious practice in that period? The answer is: much—in England, across the denominations, and elsewhere. Recent research suggests that the old picture of eighteenth-century Church of England life—low church attendance, lazy vicars, and boring liturgy—was not so much reality as a reflection of the nineteenth-century high church and evangelical historians' need to put their own innovations in a good light. The eighteenth-century church was still a focus for the identity of a parish and thereby a community where, as one observer put it, 'the whole village meet together with their best faces and in their cleanliest habits'. Undergirding this public community ritual were family devotions and private Bible reading. Collections of sermons, books like Robert Nelson's *A Companion for the Festivals and Fasts of the Church of England* (reprinted numerous times throughout the eighteenth century), and other books based on the Book of Common Prayer and the liturgical year were consistent sellers. A practical Christianity prevailed which involved good works and charity, the promotion of Christian knowledge, and rigorous moral standards. For some, virtue came to reside in charitable acts and benevolence, rather than in any specific set of theological beliefs about sin, repentance, and the intercession of Christ.

The mid-century Methodist revival has often been seen as a reaction to a dull and ineffective Church of England. Undoubtedly, John Wesley and his fellow preachers captured hearts and minds through their preaching about salvation where a reasonable, practical Christianity failed. They were adept at reaching those in the newly expanding urban and industrialized areas where the Church of England as yet had few parish churches. They were also willing to employ unusual methods of evangelism: open-air preaching and a form of door-to-door cottage evangelism at which women preachers were particularly skilled. Nevertheless this revival was not so much a reaction to a moribund Anglicanism—after all, Wesley and his followers borrowed many of their practices—religious societies, singing, and strict moral discipline—directly from the Church of England (and Wesley remained a member of the Church of England all his life, the formal Methodist split not occurring until after his death). Rather we need to put Methodism into a pan-European and transatlantic context of religious revivals which stressed a 'religion of the heart' or affective piety.

Various forms of this affective piety, both Roman Catholic and Protestant, had been developing across Europe in the seventeenth and early eighteenth centuries. Seventeenth-century France had witnessed the rise of a morally rigorous spirituality which went under the name of Jansenism, and in several Roman Catholic countries (France, Spain, Italy) a more mystical form of piety, called Quietism, developed. For Quietists, the soul is completely passive in God, and all human activity is a hindrance to communication with God.

Both Jansenism and Quietism ran into trouble with the institutional Roman Catholic church for their innovations in religious practice and spirituality. Meanwhile, Protestant piety was developing in a number of significant ways too: late seventeenth-century England witnessed a shift in Puritan piety towards the affective and emotional, as evidenced in Bunyan's writings and the many Protestant spiritual autobiographies of the period. Lutheran pietism also underwent many significant changes, not least amongst the Moravians. The key figure here was Nickolaus Zinzendorf who emphasized the experiential nature of faith. In this way, the Moravians came to downplay the religious controversies of the past and the significance of denominational differences, for the emphasis was on a person's present experience of Christ.

By the opening decades of the eighteenth century, then, most religious communities in western Europe had been affected, and in many cases renewed, by some form of spirituality which emphasized a religion not of the mind but of the heart. The Methodist revival in England tapped into this European-wide phenomenon. Travelling as missionaries to Georgia in North America, in 1735, John and Charles Wesley met with Moravian missionaries. Returning to London in 1738, the Wesleys connected with Moravians there and both John and Charles came to experience the assurance of pardon that the Moravians and other Pietists stressed. As John Wesley recorded in his diary, of his famous Aldersgate experience, he felt his 'heart strangely warmed' and an assurance that Christ had taken away 'my sins, even mine, and saved me from the law of sin and death'.

A religious revival was also underway in North America,

and this too influenced—and was influenced by—the Methodist revival in England: John and Charles Wesley and George Whitefield all travelled to America several times as missionaries, and Whitefield in particular undertook many preaching tours there. The first Great Awakening swept through the colonies in the middle decades of the eighteenth century. Doctrinal diversity and international contacts characterized the revival, influenced as it was by pietism from Germany, Calvinism from New England, Scotland, and the Netherlands, and Wesleyan Arminianism from England. 'Private letters from ministers to each other, read at public occasions on both sides of the Atlantic, created a "concert of prayer" that made the revivals of the 1740s and 1750s seem even more momentous than they were.'[5] The methods of religious renewal included itinerant preaching which appealed to the heart, harnessing popular questions about life and death to religious practice, and tapping people's yearning for miraculous and supernatural intervention. The roots of dramatic televangelism, so popular in late twentieth-century North America, might well be found in the activities of preachers such as the Tennent brothers in the mid eighteenth century.

Gilbert, John, and William Jr. Tennent, Presbyterian ministers of congregations in Philadelphia and New Jersey, all claimed to experience supernatural possession, visions, and miracles, and explained them as evidence of demonstrations of God's direct intervention in human affairs. Gilbert developed a debilitating illness and likened his recovery to the raising of Lazarus. John pleaded for and received visions of Christ during an illness. William Jr. became seriously ill while studying for his ordination examinations and was declared dead, after which he was laid out on a board for three days. His funeral was announced, at which point he opened his eyes, groaned, and was nursed back to health. Some years later, he woke up in the middle of the night to discover that the toes on one foot had dropped off, apparently without explanation—except that of perverse miracle. All of these stories provided rich material not only for their evangelical preaching but also for numerous transatlantic religious publications.[6]

This was not the only sort of religious impulse at play in eighteenth-century America. Indeed, it was a far cry from the rational stance on religion which the founding fathers took a few decades later, after the American Revolution, when they drew up the Declaration of Independence. Influenced by the ideas of English and French Enlightenment philosophers, the leading figures of late eighteenth-century America believed, rather idealistically, that a combination of Reason and freedom of religious thought and practice—which entailed the separation of church and state—would ensure that rational Christianity prevailed. Thomas Jefferson, America's third president, wrote in his *Notes on Virginia* (1787) that

Reason and free enquiry are the only effectual agents against error. Give a loose rein to them, they will support the true religion, by bringing every false one to their tribunal, to the test of their investigation. They are the natural enemies of error, and of error only.

He continued: 'Reason and experiment have been indulged, and error has fled before them. It is error alone which needs the support of government. Truth can stand by itself.' Writing in 1803 to the Philadelphia physician and political leader, Benjamin Rush, Jefferson declared himself opposed to 'the corruptions of Christianity . . . but not to the genuine precepts of Jesus himself. I am a Christian, in the only sense he wished any one to be.' Benjamin Franklin, in a letter to Ezra Stiles, the President of Yale College, in 1790 wrote something similar: 'As to Jesus of Nazareth, my opinion of whom you particularly desire, I think the system of morals and his religion, as he left them to us, the best the world ever saw or is likely to see; but I apprehend it has received various corrupting changes.'

Jefferson and Franklin were both expressing the idea, first developed by the English deists writing a hundred years before them, in the 1690s, that Christianity had been corrupted by the *institutions* of Christianity—particularly priests, who came in for a lot of insults—but that a person operating with their powers of Reason would be able to find the true core of Christianity, not least in Jesus' moral teachings. Jesus, restored to a realistic history, could provide a rational, ethical framework for life. This reduced Christianity to an ethical system, with little or no appeal to spirituality or religious practice. This academic perspective was developed throughout the eighteenth century by scholars, particularly in England, who attempted to forge a historical and critical approach to biblical texts; this approach would, of course, result in the historical Jesus movement in early nineteenth-century Germany. For some, in the eighteenth century, this historical Jesus was not necessarily divine—Franklin wrote in his letter to Stiles: 'I have, with most of the dissenters in England, some doubts as to his [Jesus'] divinity.'[7] He was alluding of course to the Unitarians, the group of dissenters which emerged in eighteenth-century England and whose religious and political ideas were deeply intertwined, as can be seen in the radical writings of both William Godwin and Mary Wollstonecraft at the end of the century.

Jefferson and Franklin may have had fine-sounding Enlightenment ideals about political and religious freedom, but such ideals did not cover the whole population. Paradoxes about identity and religion were at the very heart of America from its founding as a political entity in the eighteenth century, paradoxes which the current multi-cultural United States have yet to resolve. The case of slavery exemplifies this. America, built on Enlightenment ideals, deliberately excluded one group in particular from its declared freedoms and rights: that is, African slaves, upon whose labour the country's early wealth was largely built. Brought to America by force, they could never be a part of the immigrant, melting-pot ideal held so dear by Americans. Their inclusion in the history of eighteenth-century American Christianity therefore complicates the usual narration of that religious history in terms of pluralism and toleration.

Perhaps we should not be surprised at this exclusion, for at the very heart of Enlightenment philosophy lay the implicit belief that not everyone was quite as rational as everyone else. Sometimes this view was made explicit. David Hume wrote in 1742,

I am apt to suspect the negroes and in general all the other species of men (for there are four or five different kinds) to be naturally inferior to the whites. There never was a civilized nation of any other complexion than white, nor even any individual eminent in either action or speculation.[8]

Immanuel Kant, in his *Observations on the Feeling of the Beautiful and the Sublime* of 1764, wrote of the differences he perceived to exist between the races, and quoted Hume with approval. He wrote of a fellow who 'was quite black from head to foot, a clear proof that what he said was stupid'. And he used his crude understanding of some African religious practices to make his judgements about a black person's inferiority.

So fundamental is the difference between these two races of man, and it appears to be as great in regard to mental capacities as in colour. The religion of fetishes so widespread among them [Africans] is perhaps a sort of idolatry that sinks as deeply into the trifling as appears to be possible to human nature. A bird's feather, a cow's horn, a conch shell, or any other common object, as soon as it becomes consecrated by a few words, is an object of veneration and of invocation in swearing oaths. The blacks are very vain but in the Negro's way, and so talkative that they must be driven apart from each other with thrashings.[9]

In the institution of American slavery, slaves were indeed driven apart from each other by thrashings and African religion was suppressed. Much of this was achieved through the inculcation of a Christianity of obedience. The renowned Yale historian, Jon Butler, in his study of American Christianity in this period, notes that the rise in slave ownership by colonists paralleled a resurgence in institutional Christianity in the colonies after 1680, so that Christianity and colonial slavery shaped each other in powerful ways.

After 1680 Christianity molded the kind of slavery that touched so much in American society of the eighteenth century and later. Led by Anglicans and later powerfully reinforced by Presbyterian, Baptist and Methodist leaders, clergymen articulated a planter ethic of absolute slave obedience.

Butler calls this an 'African spiritual holocaust' which 'forever destroyed traditional African religious systems'.[10]

The white ministers who came to the plantations preached on the Pauline injunction that slaves should be obedient to their masters. Anglicans in the southern colonies were particularly prominent in developing the idea that Christianity made slaves more dutiful and loyal, so that the Christianization of slaves was urged as a matter of expedience. If Africans would agree 'in the same faith and Worship with us' then slaves would 'imbibe an everlasting Motive to Civil Unity'. These words came from Thomas Secker in his 1741 SPG (Society for the Propagation of the Gospel) sermon; he was sure that 'proper' Christian teaching relieved slaves of their rebellious instincts. His text for that sermon was Mark 6: 34—'They were as sheep not having a shepherd: and [Jesus] began to teach them many things'—which he interpreted as meaning that Christ's principal teaching was about the subjection of subordinates. Or, as he put it, the Gospel taught that rather than 'making any Alteration in Civil Rights . . . every Man abide in the Condition wherein he is called, with great Indifference of Mind concerning outward Circumstances.'[11] Secker was later to become Archbishop of Canterbury and has been described as a man 'who stood for tolerance and good sense in general'.[12]

If we are to understand that there was an underside to that Enlightenment 'tolerance and good sense' then we must also see the ways in which Christianity itself was open to multiple interpretations. Slave owners worried that Christianity's potential social effects would make slaves 'uppity' or 'proud' so that the Maryland and Virginia Assemblies had to assure potential slaveholders that slave baptisms would not abolish the servitude or labour of the Africans they purchased. Some ministers attempted to address this problem in their own distinctive ways. One Francis Le Jau, a former Huguenot turned Anglican clergyman, working amongst English planters in South Carolina, devised a baptism ritual in which he gathered all the slaves in the beautiful neo-classical parish church of St James Goose Creek (built in 1708) and required them to repeat an oath before they were baptized, 'that you do not ask for the holy baptism out of any design to free yourself from the Duty and Obedience you owe to your master while you live'.[13]

What Le Jau and others realized, at least at some unconscious level, was that baptizing slaves into Christianity was a spiritual time bomb. The white ministers might preach obedience in this world and salvation in the next, but such control is never total. Once slaves were given the tools of Christianity they adapted the religion to their own understanding. Very soon, an underground slave Christianity developed which understood Paul's more egalitarian statements, such as that in Galatians 3: 28—'there is no longer Jew or Greek, there is no longer slave or free, there is no longer male or female; for all of you are one in Jesus Christ'—to hold the promise of liberation from their present condition in *this* world. The Exodus story was passed along in oral tradition, and in slave songs and spirituals. A master might be happy that slaves were singing while they worked, but he might not have been so happy if he had heard *what* they were singing: songs which were 'pervaded by a sense of change, transcendence, ultimate justice, and personal worth', which married African musical and cultural forms to an emancipatory Christianity.[14] It was illegal for slaves to learn to read and write, but secret night-time meetings organized by the slaves themselves served as opportunities for the preaching of their own Christianity and the teaching of basic literacy skills to one another.

Christianity as it was developed by the slaves was passionate, deep in its spirituality, earthed in music, dance, and shouting. God was present and that was an ecstatic experience. In short, this Christianity was utterly incarnational, based on a strong, personal relationship with Jesus. Not surprisingly, when a further wave of evangelical revival hit America in the 1780s and 1790s, black Americans, both slave and free, converted to Christianity in larger numbers than ever before. This black Christianity was not about ethics or rules or obligations: it was about the incarnate God and the freedom he promised to his followers. It was this embodied, incarnational Christianity—*not* the watered-down version of Christianity, the rational, ethical system apparently built on Jesus' moral teachings, which Franklin, Jefferson, and other founding fathers propounded—which inspired the possibility of real political freedom. It was the intense and personal spirituality at the heart of this black Christianity which provided not only the impulse for survival of intolerable conditions, but also the hope that one might be freed from them here and now. If Jesus could save you, then he could SAVE you.

By the late eighteenth century, a transatlantic political and religious movement to abolish slavery was underway amongst white Christians of various denominations, and amongst slaves themselves. White and black Christians, women and men, slave and free, joined together to form abolition societies, political pressure groups, to end the slave trade and ultimately slavery itself. Undergirding this political movement were many deep currents of spirituality—whether the passionate black Christianity which I have just described, the intense desire to improve society and save souls for the Lord, which drove William Wilberforce and other evangelicals, or the quietly meditative but radical politics of the Quakers. Central to the abolition movement were the narratives of slaves, published and disseminated widely. Stories of conversion were often at the heart of these narratives, as in *The Interesting Narrative of the Life of Olaudah Equiano* published in 1792. It was the terrible experience of slavery, told first-hand by those who had experienced it, which was employed to win hearts and therefore minds. Here, in these slave narratives, an appeal to experience, an Enlightenment principle gleaned from Locke, joined with an appeal to the heart, a principle gleaned from the effective spirituality of the period, to convert the reader to the abolitionist cause—and in the process prove that blacks could read, write, and had an intelligence and dignity equal to that of whites.

However, a legacy of this piece of eighteenth-century history is a tension at the heart of African-American culture about the role of Christianity. Undoubtedly, 'black church' has been absolutely central to African-American culture, for a long time being one of the few public institutions in which blacks could serve, speak publicly, and engage in political activism, as well as acting as a support base for a repeatedly marginalized ethnic group. And yet the shadow remains: Christianity was largely forced upon the African population in eighteenth-century North America, even if that population simultaneously turned it to liberatory ends. The ensuing tension is epitomized in the differences between Martin Luther King Jr, Baptist minister and leader of the non-violent civil-rights movement of the 1950s and 60s, and Malcolm X, convert to Islam, who felt that Christianity was always and could only ever be the white man's oppressive religion. This tension remains in black theology today.

Undoubtedly, paradoxes have always existed within Christianity about the equality of human beings. Jesus' teachings seem to promise equality for all, but the epistles of Paul, addressed to specific social situations, have repeatedly been taken as caveats on that equality. The Enlightenment's talk of universal rights—which maybe were not so universal—complicated this picture even further. We see it, for example, in the political debates and philosophical writings leading up to and during the French Revolution with regard to women. The outbreak of the French Revolution in 1789 was seen by many as the culmination of Enlightenment ideals, especially in the Declaration of the Rights of Man and the Citizen, approved by the French National Assembly on 27 August 1789, which embodied the notion that by employing Reason society could be improved.

The National Assembly recognizes and proclaims, in the presence and under the auspices of the Supreme Being, the following rights of man and citizen:
1. Men are born and remain free and equal in rights; social distinction may be based only upon general usefulness.
2. The aim of every political association is the preservation of the natural and inalienable rights of man; these rights are liberty, property, security and resistance to oppression.

The question was: did 'man' stand for man, or for human being? Was the term to be used in its particular or universal form? Two years later, in 1791, as political events were hotting up but women seemed not yet to be enjoying any greater freedom, this was the question posed by Olympe de Gouges. Putting forward a Declaration of the Rights of Woman and the Female Citizen, she rewrote the preamble and first two articles thus:

The sex that is as superior in beauty as it is in courage during the sufferings of maternity recognizes and declares in the presence and under the auspices of the Supreme Being, the following rights of Woman and of Female Citizens.

1. Woman is born free and lives equal to man in her rights. Social distinctions can be based only on the common utility.

2. The purpose of any political association is the conservation of the natural and imprescriptible rights of woman and man; these rights are liberty, property, security, and especially resistance to oppression.

A year later, Mary Wollstonecraft, a writer in the radical political culture of 1790s London, published her *Vindication of the Rights of Woman*. Influenced by the radical Unitarians with whom she mixed, she argued on *religious* grounds that woman should have equal rights with man, appealing, via reason, to the eternal truths of a good, wise, and reasonable God, and urging men to allow women to become what the Maker has always required them to be.

The Enlightenment promised equality and rights, but the question was and is always: to whom? Christianity as a religion has promised equality and freedom, but the question has too often been: for whom? When the Enlightenment failed certain

groups—black Americans, European and English women—
they turned to the Christian gospel's promises of freedom. In
the following two centuries, this relationship has often been
reversed. When Christianity has failed certain groups, they
have appealed to the reasonable voice of the Enlightenment
and its promise of liberty and civil rights—hence feminism
took a secular turn in the mid-twentieth century and many
current gay-rights groups reject Christianity outright. A key
legacy from the eighteenth century, at least here in the west, is
this tension, this sense of a mission left incomplete. It should
therefore come as no surprise to us that the churches and
society are today convulsed by internal conflict about issues
like gender and sexuality, racism and justice. Enlightenment
and Christian discourses about equality and rights, sometimes
in conflict with one another, at other times seen as beating
with one heart, remain profoundly unresolved.

So far, I have looked at Christian developments within
England, parts of Europe, and North America in relation to
each other. I want now to turn, briefly, to the west's relationship to the rest of the world. For eighteenth-century Christians
in the west did not only have to face the differences within, but
also those outside. This was the century in which the west came
to encounter with increasing speed other religions and cultures.
Out of this encounter came two key modern impulses: the
comparative study of religion, and the missionary movement.
The attempt to understand the *nature* of religion, as a cross-
cultural phenomenon, had begun with a number of thinkers in
the late seventeenth century and early eighteenth century, but
especially with the English deists—about whom I will talk
more in a minute—and certain French encyclopedists and

philosophers, such as Pierre Bayle. Of course, these thinkers rarely visited the cultures about which they theorized: they gleaned their knowledge from travel literature. They were, in that sense, truly armchair philosophers.

The deists combined their reading of travel literature with their own desire to understand the rational impulse which, they felt, was at the heart of all true religion. They thus compared the practices and belief systems of different religions, seeking the common denominator in all religions, a natural religious impulse, common to all places at all times. They did this by seeing what elements of other religions were like the rational form of Christianity which they considered *true* religion. So, for example, Islam was to be tolerated because it was really the same as Christianity, not least because it was monotheistic. John Toland, the English deist, wrote in his *Letters to Serena* of 1704, 'I see no reason a Christian shou'd fear to read the Alcoran [that is, the Koran] which is as true of all the Books in the world.'[15] It was true because it expressed the essentials of true Christianity. Indeed, rational Muslims could more properly be called Christians, according to this scheme of things, than could superstitious Christians (by which the deists meant Roman Catholics). The deists thus drew up two-tiered philosophies of religion. As the intellectual historian Frank Manuel writes of the deists' view:

There were two religions in every society, one for the men of reason, and one for the fanatics, one for those who comprehended the marvellous order of the world and one for those who relied on gods for every event, the ignorant men full of terrors which they allayed with ludicrous rituals.[16]

So began one strand of the modern west's long history of attempting to know the foreign, but frequently resorting to making it familiar. As Edward Said wrote in his influential book of 1978, *Orientalism*:

Something patently foreign and distant acquires, for one reason or another, a status more rather than less familiar. One tends to stop judging things either as completely novel or as completely well-known; a new median category emerges, a category that allows one to see new things, things seen for the first time, as versions of a previously known thing. In essence such a category is not so much a way of receiving new information as it is a method of controlling what seems to be a threat to some established view of things.[17]

This deist view of religion had an impact on the intellectual elite's perception of other religions when they were abroad. This is illustrated by the following comment from Lady Mary Wortley Montagu when she was living in Turkey from 1716 to 1718. 'The Turks are not so ignorant as we fancy them to be', she wrote. 'The effendis (that is to say, the learned) do very well deserve this name: they have no more faith in the inspiration of Mahomet than in the infallibility of the Pope. They make a frank profession of deism among themselves, or to those they can trust.'[18]

Eighteenth-century thinkers therefore tried to grapple with a serious epistemological problem: how to *know* another religion. Such a question was possible once the military threat from another religion had been overcome, as was the case with Islam in the west—the Turks had been defeated at Vienna in 1683. The Ottoman empire in particular, and Islamic culture in general, came to be seen as less of a threat to Europe. Islam was, therefore, no longer a heresy to be combated, as in the Middle Ages, but another religious culture to be *known*—even if that meant, as it did for the English and French philosophers, making it in their own image, and thereby colonizing it linguistically and rhetorically.

Another option was, of course, not to attempt to know the other religious culture at all, but to try and convert all non-Christians (or 'heathen', as the missionaries called them) to Christianity. Such an attitude did not, however, exclude the advances of Enlightenment thought and technology which were needed for travel, and were incorporated into the scientific knowledge and educational principles which the missionaries took with them. The modern missionary movement was Protestant in its initial impulses, growing out of the different waves of the evangelical revival which occurred throughout the eighteenth century. India, for example, received missionaries at the beginning of the century, in 1706, when Danish Protestants—supported by the English SPCK—arrived, and at the end of the century when William Carey, the famous founder of the Baptist Missionary Movement (1792), settled at Serampore. Missionary work in the non-western world was not originally self-evident: Carey was inspired, for example, by reading about Cook's journeys in the Pacific. Nevertheless, mission abroad soon became central to the late eighteenth- and early nineteenth-century evangelical revival in Britain. Following Carey's initiative, the London Missionary Society, supported by 'liberal Churchmen and conscientious Dissenters, pious Calvinists and pious Arminians', was founded in 1795, and the Church Missionary Society in 1799. The end of the eighteenth century saw beginnings of the western missionary movement which would, in the nineteenth century, join with political forces of colonization, and effect a huge transformation in—particularly—India and Africa. There is, of course, a multitude of repercussions in our own age from this missionary impulse, not least the changed face of the Anglican communion in which the average Anglican is no longer white, male, and English but black, female, and African. But how that came about is, as they say, another story—one, perhaps, for those lecturers who will follow me.

Let me now bring my own comments to a conclusion. I began this lecture by quoting the theologian Don Cupitt's version of the Enlightenment. Cupitt presented a smooth picture of progress and resolution—but also rather a 'thin' and sanitized version of the Enlightenment and Christianity in this period. My intention has been to present a quite different and rather more textured picture of Christianity in the late seventeenth and eighteenth centuries, a period of contradictory impulses which, in many ways, remain unresolved today. For the Enlightenment opened up, and yet did not solve, the question of *who* has equality and rights, *who* is perfectible, and *who*, through the power of their own thinking, can begin to understand the nature of God. It raised the question of whether that justice of which the gospel speaks is to be inspired by reason or passionate religious experience. The birth of modern science opened up the question of whether and how our ever-increasing knowledge of the world, and how it works, can be reconciled with a faith in the Christian God. At the same time, the affective piety which developed in a series of strong currents throughout the period—in various religious revivals, and in slave religion—brought alive to many the presence of God in embodied and experiential form. It seems to me—a woman and a priest, a scholar, and a person of faith—that the legacy of the Enlightenment is to ask whether we can resolve these questions, joining spirituality with the life of the mind, justice with the passionate and incarnate practice of religion, reason with equality, in our own world.

8

THE NINETEENTH CENTURY

Jane Garnett

Statistical data suggest that in 1800 the world was 23 per cent Christian (rather less than one-quarter), of which 86.5 per cent were white. By 1900 the world was 34.4 per cent Christian (rather more than one-third), of which 81 per cent were white. Given that the population of the world had vastly increased (by roughly three quarters) over this period, these figures indicate that the nineteenth century saw the fastest relative growth of the Christian churches since the earliest centuries. Yet the nineteenth century is still conventionally seen as a century of religious crisis and decline, prefiguring the more extensive processes of secularization in the twentieth century. What these figures in part hint at is the degree to which the fulcrum of active Christian participation was to shift in the twentieth century from Europe and North America to the rest of the world. Yet at the start of the twentieth century the implications of this possibility were only very indirectly acknowledged. What is striking is the fundamental maintenance, throughout the nineteenth century, of Christian confidence in western leadership and a western framework of analysis. This was self-evidently true for those who continued to rejoice in the providential harmony of Christianity, civilization, and commerce. But it was as true for those who recognized the challenges presented to the defence of Christianity by the study of comparative religion and of non-western cultures, as it was for those who were profoundly critical of many of the developments in nineteenth-century western society—the growth of materialism, the privileging of the pursuit of individual selfishness, the loss of a sense of community. Whilst Van Gogh might find inspiration in a romantic ideal of the uncorrupted spirituality and oneness with nature of the Japanese, this point of reference was for him still instrumental to the rhetoric of reforming western mores. It was a response to an assumption that Christianity defined western civilization, and that the loss of living Christian spirituality would inherently threaten the integrity of that civilization.

For nations or regions which were faced with the challenges of modernization in the late nineteenth century—Japan, India, Russia (under Orthodoxy the largest Christian culture in the world)—the question was also: does successful modernization equate with the assumption of western values? To what extent were those the values of western Christendom in the universal sense? Were they rather the values of western (specifically Protestant?) rationality, political ideology, and capitalism? For much of the twentieth century promotion of, opposition to, or embarrassment about missions and colonialism have tended to essentialize the dichotomy between west and east. Until relatively recently the sheer variety and nuances of perspective in the interaction of cultures have been obscured. Moreover, twentieth-century academic specialization has tended to divide the intellectual spheres within which nineteenth-century Christian thinkers were engaged. The origins of modern disciplinary categories have been sought, a quest which has too often involved privileging the secular side of a polemical dichotomy, which was at the time part of a much richer debate over definitions. This is true of economics, social science, psychology, all of which in the nineteenth century were areas of inquiry debated critically by Christians in the context of religious culture and moral philosophy. The Christian expansion beyond Europe and North America was not at the expense of a broader intellectual and social engagement with the challenges of modern life and modern ideas at home. It is an irony that it is partly because of the hegemony of modern western analytical assumptions—including linear models of secularization and rationalization derived from nineteenth-century thinkers, Comte, Marx, Weber, Durkheim, which were themselves highly contingent and strongly contested—that we fail to give due weight to the creative range of nineteenth-century western Christianity.

The Protestant German romantic artist Philipp Otto Runge proclaimed in 1802 that 'we stand on the edge of all religions'.[1] Out of the chaos of the French Revolution, when the old orders and values had been destroyed, he called for the artist to depict landscape 'in its paradisal totality' in order to lead people back to a sense of unity with God and with creation. Reacting against what he saw as the cool rationality and disinterested aesthetic of the late eighteenth century, he articulated in artistic terms the more general sense that the Revolution opened up the possibility of religious revival. Such romantic rhetoric, rooted in a revitalized natural theology, raised potent questions which were to be confronted in the nineteenth century. First about the relationship between, on the one hand, the general diffusion of Christian values and symbols and, on the other, the direct pursuit of Christian conversion by institutional churches. Such a distinction—indeed the possibility of posing it—is of course fundamental to an understanding of the role and achievement of Christianity. Statistics of church membership and church attendance give a very partial picture. The question was contested at the time by Christians of different theological and cultural outlooks, and was found to present particular challenges in the context both of home and overseas missions. In late nineteenth-century India liberal Protestant missionaries began to move away from conversion to seeing a congruence between Hinduism and Christianity as likely to result in a more creative role for Christian values in that particular non-western context. This was in turn challenged by the religious absolutism of zealous Keswick revivalists who in both India and Africa moved away from any such accommodation with non-Christian culture.

The second question posed by romantic rhetoric concerned the fundamental nature of Christian apologetic. The romantic emphasis on images—visual and verbal—as stimuli to the heart, the imagination, and the conscience was countered by those who argued that the only way to defend Christianity against scientific challenges was to use the weapons of the sceptics—the logic of the word. This tension could both reinforce and cut across the polarization between liberalism and dogmatism which the Revolution stimulated. It could also be played out both at the high intellectual level of argument about scientific plausibility and at a very popular level. In a period in which technological advance permitted the proliferation and rapid dissemination of images on a scale hitherto unknown, and in which religious culture was competing in an increasingly complex cultural market, the challenges to creative adaptation were multiple. The tensions have continued until now. Despite Hegelian anticipations, the nineteenth century did *not* see the triumph of the rational word over the imaginative impulse.

The revolutions at the end of the eighteenth century in first America and then France raised fundamental questions about the role of religion in society and the relationship of church and state, which were to have a much wider impact in the early nineteenth century. The spectrum of effects was broad—from a stimulus to freedom of choice and action to the impetus to violent reaction and the reassertion of authority. But even at the latter extreme control was never to be straightforward. The social and political significance of religion in the nineteenth century was in fact heightened by the *interaction* between extensive social fragmentation and the proliferation and pluralization of religious groups and movements. Religious culture was marked by strong regional particularity and often polarization. Its forms and meanings were open to debate—and change was a matter of subtle shifts of balance, not of the exclusive adoption of one or another clear-cut position, however much contemporary or subsequent rhetoric might imply that this was what was going on. A religious—or in some cases a very specifically anti-religious—position defined communal, political, and intellectual identity in increasingly sharp and intense ways in the nineteenth century—partly because it was felt that, now, fewer things could be taken for granted.

In the wake of the Revolution a campaign of dechristianization was instituted in France in 1793–4. Churches were to be transformed into temples of reason, personal and place names with religious associations were to be eliminated. However, these aspects of the campaign seem to have achieved very limited success, and, as one might expect, had most impact in those areas where religious commitment was already weakest. A single image (see Fig. 4) illuminates a more general point: that black and white oppositions between traditionalism and modernization, Christianity and dechristianization, do not begin to capture the way in which cultural developments work. The picture is on a plate produced in 1793 with the inscription 'Anne Chérot Bonne Citoyenne'. The image is of Anne Chérot's patron saint—Anne, the mother of the Virgin Mary—teaching the Virgin to read. Innumerable such plates were produced and sold to peasants, artisans, workers, and petits bourgeois, as they had been before the Revolution. They offer one vivid indication of the potential for the maintenance of Christian tradition within the new revolutionary regime—the Catholic image juxtaposed to the language of the Revolution—of good citizenship. At the same time the attack on the constitutional church, which left many parts of France without a priest at all, had significant longer-term effects on religious life and the authority of the priesthood. There was a resurgence of popular cults and forms of religious practice. Lay men and women even began to take over the functions of the priest and to say Masses. This appropriation of religious authority by lay people was to remain a potent weapon in dealing with the church hierarchy. After 1820 one community resorted to holding lay assemblies when their campaign for separate parish status was refused by their bishop. Women were particularly prominent in the maintenance and regeneration of popular religion, starting a trend which was to become more marked over the century. Similar developments were to be apparent in many of the Italian and German states in the same period. In Latin America the first decades of the nineteenth century saw a series of revolutions establishing independence from Spanish or Portuguese rule. In their wake there was a shortage of clergy and no bishops were initially appointed. When a firmly ultramontane hierarchy was reimposed, it sat at a considerable imaginative distance from the flourishing rural Catholic culture which both continued and reinvented its own creative synthesis between Christian and older indigenous traditions. San Isidro the Farmer—a twelfth-century Spanish saint—was transposed into the minute detail of the agricultural landscape of mid-nineteenth-century Bolivia. A Corpus Christi mask from nineteenth-century Ecuador represented a blending of Andean and Catholic symbols and aesthetics: the sunburst form provided a reminiscence both of the Inca solstice and of the Catholic monstrance; small Christian reliquaries were incorporated amongst figures of animals, notably sheep, important both in Christian and Andean iconography.

The Catholic revival which the hierarchy encouraged over the course of the nineteenth century retained its popular dimension. Although the institutional church gained increasing confidence, and the papacy was to become associated by its opponents with the worst sort of clerical authoritarianism, the effect of this was more ideological than tangible in many local Catholic contexts. In the entire Catholic world new lay fraternities sprang up, as well as new religious congregations sponsored by the church. Some of these fraternities competed directly with secular social clubs and appealed to particular groups—mothers and young men and women especially. The proliferation of societies dedicated to St Vincent de Paul built on a recognition of the gap between the rhetoric of progress and the reality of great social and economic inequalities. These societies ministered specifically to the poor and provided assistance to those hit by fluctuations in the capitalist economy. French and German socialism in the 1840s and 1850s was itself strongly infused with Christian ideas, which gave a moral strength to artisan and peasant politicization. Primitive Christianity was appealed to by Etienne Cabet as authority for his Christian communism. Specifically Catholic mutual aid societies dedicated to local saints were set up both to reinforce and to transform moral values so as to enable members to meet the challenges of an increasingly complex market culture. Local cults were promoted and supported by lay people in ways which the church as an institution frequently opposed and then tried retrospectively to pick up on.

It is well known that the cult of Mary experienced a

dramatic revival in the nineteenth century, symbolized by Pius IX's enunciation of the doctrine of the Immaculate Conception in 1854. But the official promotion of the cult as a universal one represented an attempt to control and to benefit from a proliferation of local Marian revivals, some of which sat less than comfortably with papal authority. The Virgin of Guadalupe, supported by local priests and laity, was appointed guardian of the rebellion of Hidalgo in Mexico in 1810, and local Madonnas played varied roles in the revolutions of 1848–9 in Europe. There was a growing number of Marian apparitions in the period after the French Revolution. In France there had been officially recognized appearances— in 1830–31 in Paris, in 1846 in La Salette, and in 1858 in Lourdes, and a whole host had never received official sanction. The apparitions had a powerful and uncontrollable popular dimension. When the Virgin appeared in Paris in 1830 she asked that medals should be struck with her image on them. By 1842 *100 million medals* had been produced, and miraculous cures were reported in connection with many of them. Sociologically, there seem to be many common factors: the visionaries were predominantly poor, often rural and female—in various respects marginal to the dominant culture. The number of apparitions increased at times of economic distress and political crisis—the 1790s, the 1830s in France, 1848–9, and the 1860s and 1870s in the German and Italian states, where they engaged specifically with the rhetoric of nation-building. The enemy against whom the Virgin was to intercede was usually the liberal anticlericalism which was defining the state in Germany, Italy, and France. In Marpingen, a village in the Saarland, where three young girls saw an apparition of the Virgin in 1876, the whole affair seemed to liberal commentators an affront to the new state, which they constructed as liberal, masculine, rational, and Protestant. Given the particular involvement of women—in claiming to see the visions in the first place, and then in visiting the site, gender sharpened the rhetorical weapons: 'Under the sign of exorcisms, stigmatic women, and apparitions of the Virgin, the ultramontanes propose to vanquish the spirit of the nineteenth century.'[2]

This way of framing such phenomena underlines the degree to which religious commitments were engaging in a newly charged political and economic context. But there were also important devotional continuities, as there were to be into the twentieth century. Even more extensive in their impact than the cults of apparitions were the innumerable local cults of miracle-working images of the Virgin throughout the urban and rural Catholic world, as also in the Orthodox world. In most cases these cults and the new miracles recorded represented the revitalization of a much older tradition, although in some cases—as in the Virgin set into an apartment block in the new middle-class extension to late nineteenth-century Genoa—a new cult was created to sacralize a new urban space. It is clear from certain miracle stories that even a cheap, mass-reproduced copy of an image could be held to be charged with the same potency as its prestigious original—a development which was not always welcomed by the clergy, who could sense a dangerous loss of control, or by some Catholic intellectuals, who found the proliferation of what they saw as kitsch or sentimental piety distasteful and undermining to a proper sense of religious dignity. However, printed reproductions were used as aids to devotion by all social groups in church, and in the home, where they were displayed in ways which bear significant comparison with the 'beautiful corner' where Orthodox Russians have traditionally set icons in their houses. A cheap tinted print on paper of the Madonna of Montebruno in Liguria (Italy) (see Fig. 5) was framed with card, on which were stuck shells, pieces of coral, and angels from commercial Christmas decorations; the Virgin and Child were crowned with pieces of silver paper. Many nineteenth-century reproductions were made for households of Our Lady of Kozelschana, an icon clearly derived from Italian renaissance models, which performed a series of miraculous healings in Moscow in the 1880s. In the context of mass migration from Catholic Europe to North and South America, image cults were transferred. Frequently a copy of the original image was commissioned and erected in the new settlement. At the same time, close contact was maintained with the source, whether through pilgrimage home; through correspondence, in which miracles worked by the now venerated copy were reported; or through the sending of ex-votos to the original image (see Fig. 6: an ex-voto from newly arrived migrants to Argentina to the Madonna of Montallegro, above Rapallo). Such cults were never susceptible to clerical appropriation, and provided a powerful focus for the creation of a sense of communal identity in a new setting. In an Italian quarter of New York in 1899, it was reported that the members of a mutual benefit society preferred to have the statue of their patron saint set up in a saloon, where they could keep an eye on it, rather than in the church.

In Protestant Britain and North America the early nineteenth century saw a religious revival which in some respects was a continuation of eighteenth-century evangelical awakening, but which took more varied forms and confronted challenges of urbanization and commercialization on a new scale. It was the very vitality of these revivals—especially those in commercial communities on both sides of the Atlantic in 1859–60 and in the early 1870s, and those associated with the Keswick conferences from 1875 which provided stimuli to missionary activity. In America this revival took place in a religious free market in which the Arminian evangelical churches challenged not just Anglican episcopalianism, but also elements of the older puritan tradition. White respectability was challenged by those Methodist and Baptist camp meetings characterized by jumping, shouting, and dancing, which brought elements of Methodist worship which had always been controversial into creative combination with Indian and African performance tradition. Such a model of religious experience was to provide the basis for the development of the Holiness and Pentecostal movements in the later part of the century—and was to continue to prove uncomfortable for those still keen to defend Protestantism on the ground of its explicability in the terms of scientific rationality. This had both a social and a gender dimension: Methodism and Pentecostalism appealed particularly to women and to black communities.

In Britain the question of the relationship of the church to the state remained constitutive of debate about the nature of a Christian society. Although the Anglican church was only disestablished in Ireland during this period, it was operating in

England and Wales in a profoundly new competitive climate. The constitutional changes of 1828–9 raised questions at all levels about the nature of Anglican authority, and prompted intense intra-Anglican activity and conflict at a time of rising nonconformist competition. Anglican culture in England retained a significant cultural status, although Arnoldian formulations of its generalized role were to come under sustained attack by the defenders of dogmatic authority. Protestantism broadly defined British identity, only being strongly contested in Ireland, but this was a Protestantism whose varieties of emphasis and different historical traditions were crucial to the sustained vitality of that Britishness in particular places. This was especially to be noted in the imperial and missionary context, in the energy for example given to the establishment of distinct types of Protestant community under the aegis of Scottish presbyterian and English Anglican settlers in New Zealand.

Both the rhetoric and the reality of the varieties of English-speaking Protestantism were of course in fundamental ways distinct from those of their Catholic counterparts. But perhaps in more ways than any would have recognized at the time there could be points of affinity both in their shaping of a response to the intellectual challenges of the day and in their practical engagement with modern life. One of the key developments of the nineteenth century was the expansion of market capitalism, which both provided models and opportunities for more effective inter-church competition, and also presented hazards for the maintenance of Christian values and Christian community. At a practical level Protestant religious groups organized themselves into societies and targeted sections of society particularly vulnerable to the pressures of the market, just as Catholics did. Both single and married women took on significant roles in Protestant associational culture, and introduced innovation in devotional practice. They took a particularly key position in overseas mission, especially in India and China where male missionaries could not have dealings with high-status women. The missionary women constructed an idea of such women as being both central to and degraded by their non-western society, on the forcefully argued basis that women constituted the foundation of any civilized society. In so doing, of course, they provided ideological support for their own position.

Protestants responded energetically to the opportunities presented by cheap publishing and advertising. There was an explosion of religious periodicals and devotional literature of all sorts. Catholic saints were remodelled in Protestant terms, and an exhaustive project of commemorating Protestant heroes of past or present was embarked upon. In 1825 the American Tract Society was formed—a merger of forty smaller societies. By 1827 it had printed over 3 million items, by 1828 over 5 million. The best artists and engravers were employed to provide images. In both Britain and North America there was a vast proliferation of Bibles and portions of the Bible, adapted for different markets, many of which were illustrated. Between 1808 and 1901 the British and Foreign Bible Society produced over 46 million Bibles, 71 million New Testaments and nearly 53 million sections of Scripture. Clearly the emphasis on the availability of Scripture was a particularly Protestant preoccupation, and Protestants were to the fore in Bible translation into other languages in this period. In 1800 printed Scriptures were available in 67 languages; by 1900 in 537. The *creative* role of missionaries in this context has recently received its due emphasis. In order to prepare the ground for the impact of vernacular Scripture, dictionaries and grammars had to be constructed, which in the most fundamental sense established a medium of communication in which the indigenous people took priority. This also, of course, in the best cases had the effect of refining western missionaries' sense of the particularity of local definitions of culturally crucial concepts. The Basel missionary Johannes Christaller spent thirty years in Ghana preparing a dictionary and also a massive compilation of proverbs and idioms of Akan culture.

In other respects dynamic Protestants moved on to comparable ground to that worked by Catholics, although the fruits of their efforts looked very different. Whilst Protestants (and not just Calvinists) still derided Catholicism as a religion of the imagination, increasing use was made of visual imagery, whether in devotional or advice literature or in the material of sermons. The Calvinist American artist Frederick Church exhibited in 1857 a gigantic painting of the Niagara Falls, attracting 100,000 paying spectators in two weeks. Commercially marketed reproductions were promoted as 'silent, beautiful sermons'. Nonconformists in Britain came to draw on Ruskin's art criticism to support readings both of landscape painting and of works representing biblical figures and narratives, although issues of biblical representation remained a matter of controversy (relating closely to debates on how the Bible should be read textually). In the latter half of the century the Pre-Raphaelites came to be colonized in safe Protestant terms. One Welsh minister preaching to a predominantly middle-class congregation in London and publishing his addresses first in a religious periodical and then in the 1880s as a separate book, drew his themes from famous modern paintings. His assumption was that his congregation and readers would know these paintings—presumably for the most part through reproduction—and would be able to call significant details to mind. Alongside such developments ran the reproduction of more conservative text-dominated images drawn from an older Protestant tradition of emblem books. One of the most celebrated of these was the 'broad and narrow way' chromo-lithographic print which depicted an allegorical landscape with two paths: Sunday school and the deaconess institute provide stations on the way to heaven; the theatre and the Sunday train offer transport to hell. Biblical references explicate the image at every salient point (see Fig. 7). It was designed in Stuttgart in 1862, a Dutch edition was produced in 1866, a copy of which was brought back to Britain by Gawin Kirkham in 1868. From an enlarged version he was said to have lectured more than 1,100 times before his death in 1892.

Attendance at public lectures on every conceivable subject and geared for different social and intellectual levels was a hugely popular activity, and all religious groups were aware of the need to choreograph the occasion to make an impact, just as did scientific demonstrators or straightforward entertainers. Lantern slides of Christian subjects were used to create theatrical effects, in which images, stories, and music were often combined in complex multi-sensory performances. The technology had improved to the point where the effects did indeed seem magical or miraculous. There were mechanical slides in which the images seemed to move, and so-called 'dissolving views' where one image slowly dissolved into another. Such magic lanterns came also to be used for services, and were taken on missions at home and abroad. David Livingstone never travelled without one, and the Revd George Allchin claimed to have staged 357 shows in Japan in the 1890s. A potent combination of western imagery, technology, and religion was projected in the metaphor of enlightenment. One American clergyman wrote in the 1890s of having a parish which demanded 'all that ingenuity and industry can produce to secure and retain enthusiasm in religious matters'.[3] He made his own slides, carried his camera everywhere, and wrote his sermons from the stimulus of the images. A description of the parish church of St Mary-at-Hill in the City of London in the same period noted the determination of the rector—the Secretary of the Church Army—to adapt some of the methods of the Salvation Army to the Church of England to enhance its popularity amongst the working classes. His efforts were described (with no particular hostility) as sensationalist. The lantern service, which replaced evensong, was the high point, a large white sheet being suspended from the chancel arch and enormous images being projected from the organ loft. He also advertised in the press topical themes on which he was to preach, and before the Sunday evening service processed through the streets with a group of singers to drum up custom. While this was going on, a sacred concert with dissolving views was taking place in the church. The result was a packed church; and, as the commentator added, 'That the right sort of people are attracted is shown by the burglar's picklock and empty whisky bottle that were lately left in the pews'.[4]

It was perhaps appropriate that one of the most popular of lantern slides was Holman Hunt's *Light of the World* (see Fig. 8). In its original version, painted in 1853, it received a lukewarm critical reception, partly because it seemed too emotionally immediate and intense. But this quality, together with its symbolism, made it an ideal lantern image and focus for sermon exposition. It was in fact in response to being told of such a use of the image that Hunt made (private) reference to his own sense that he had painted it with what he had felt to be divine command. A later large-scale version of the painting was sent on a hugely successful tour of the British Empire, as an extraordinary realization of the metaphor which the painting embodies. Whether on tour, in the form of lantern projections, or printed reproduction, people commented that it showed Christ 'as they had imagined him to be'. This was both a real tribute to the resonances of this particular image, and also a reflection of the late nineteenth-century Protestant desire to objectify an image of Christ. (This goal was often expressed in explicit contradistinction to Marian imagery, which was criticized for its proliferation and for never establishing a unitary *type*.) Ironically over-exposure to this single image through mass reproduction was ultimately to make it seem hackneyed and indeed inappropriate, but this only occurred well into the twentieth century.

The range of such cultural manifestations could seem exhilarating, or it could seem dangerously close to selling out to the spectacular demands of modern capitalism—the adoption of the superficial rhetoric of advertising, and the failure to maintain the essential quality of what was being promoted. Protestants were anxious that they were more vulnerable to this charge than Catholics, partly in so far as the intimate relationship between Protestant values and capitalist progress was so much taken as a commonplace. Had Protestant culture in other respects become commercialized? Had Protestants indeed traded on their Protestantism in their commercial transactions to the point where the evident pursuit of self-interest showed that Protestantism to be a debased currency? This question was posed with particular sharpness in relation to missionary endeavour which could be seen to run too obviously alongside commercial activity. But it was a question posed more generally as part of an important strand of Protestant self-criticism over the second half of the nineteenth century. Since Protestantism was defined in relation to its global economic role, a clearer understanding of the complexities of religious and moral responsibility was crucial if the constructive role of that Protestantism was to be fully attained.

A Protestant ethic needed to be constructed rather than assumed. The construction of this ethic became associated with the revival of Protestant moral philosophy in reaction to materialism and positivism. It also confronted arguments for Christianity which had become so abstract as to deny the real challenges of faith, and the moral and spiritual need for a secure sense of personal engagement with Christ. Such arguments included those presented by Henry Longueville Mansel in his famous Bampton Lectures, published in 1859 as *The Limits of Religious Thought*, which provoked Newman's comment that 'to assert that nothing is known because nothing is know luminously and exactly seems to me saying that we do not see the stars because we cannot tell their number, size or distance from each other'.[5] Mansel's argument for the unknowability of God rested on a view of reason so narrow as to be completely sterile. The Gospels contained not philosophy but the recognizable reality of Christ's life. In British, North American, German, and French Protestant cultures in the last quarter of the nineteenth century there was a revived incarnationalism and preoccupation with Christian social ethics. At the same time developments in psychology offered new ways of addressing the question how the reality of religious experience could be distinguished and endorsed, and of refuting the predominantly agnostic anthropological view that any form of spiritualism was an atavistic survival in modern society. In Britain and America the study of psychology was still institutionally related to philosophy, and hence could contribute, as William James centrally did, to the philosophy of religion by recognizing the wider dimensions of human experience of which religion formed a dynamic part. The last two decades of the century saw (briefly) a greater openness to scientific agnosticism in reaction to positivistic argument.

In this context both Protestants and Catholics attacked the notion of examining the economy as an autonomous sphere of human activity. In challenging the premises either of Protestant liberal culture or of secular liberal culture Catholics affirmed the interlocking religious and economic virtues of loyalty, reciprocity, and altruism in place of individualistic competitive dogmas. In doing so they tried to recapture the traditions of Catholic philosophy interrupted by Protestant rationalism. The renewed authority given to Aquinas and through him to Aristotle reinforced the making of a distinction between the worth of actions in terms of the end pursued. This could radically confront conventional economic validations of work in terms of the production simply of exchange-values in the market. The reinforcement of the role of Catholic devotional life in modern civil society was seen to be inherently related to this. Because in no context was nineteenth-century Catholicism in an economically hegemonic position, it was easier in some ways for the Catholic approach to retain a clearer critical thrust into the twentieth century. Catholic culture, too, which seemed to secularists to represent the most backward form of religious survival, was able to retain its communal identity more readily. But the fact that the Protestant path was in many ways more prone to assimilation to the values of the modern capitalist world should not obscure the creative ways in which Protestants resisted that identification in the nineteenth century. Neither Catholics nor Protestants succeeded in fundamentally transforming the methodology of economics, which was to develop within a narrower disciplinary frame in the twentieth century. But the continued posing of critical questions framed by an increasingly dynamic Christian culture was both constitutive of confidence in those cultural values and also helped to reinforce a practical protest against the artificial fragmentation of modes of understanding the human condition. In these terms lay the imaginative impact of nineteenth-century Western Christianity as both culture and counter-culture.

Figure 4. Anne Chérot Bonne Citoyenne. Courtesy of the Collection Louis Heitschel, Saint-Germain-en-Laye, France.

Figure 5. Madonna of Montebruno, Liguria, Italy. Nineteenth-century tinted engraving, framed with shells, coral, and commercial Christmas decorations on card. Courtesy of Anselmo Crovaro, Manarola, Italy.

FICALLO EMANUELLE E FRANCESCO COSTA, MARIA COSTA PER MEMORIA DI GRAZIA OTTENVTA DALLA N.S. DI MONTE ALLEGRO L'12 MARZO 1871 IN BUENOSAIRES.

Figure 6. *Ex-voto* oil painting to the Madonna of Montallegro, Rapallo, Italy (nineteenth century). Courtesy of Santuario di Montallegro, Rapallo.

Figure 7. 'The Broad and the Narrow Way.' Nineteenth-century chromolithograph.

Figure 8. W. Holman Hunt, *The Light of the World* (1851–3). Courtesy of the Warden and Fellows of Keble College, Oxford.

9

THE TWENTIETH CENTURY

Adrian Hastings

When reflecting on the achievement and lasting significance of any earlier century, one has the considerable advantage not only of distance, but also of knowledge of a subsequent century against which to examine one's own subject. For the twentieth we do not have this. Hence it remains not only the clearest in our minds, given that we have all experienced a part of it and have a far greater mountain of available information than for any previous one, but also the obscurest. The nearer we are to now, the less we can be sure about which way the train is going and what will be its next stop. Without some knowledge of the hereafter, information about the nearly present is almost unassessable in terms of its real significance.

In 1910 a Glebo Episcopalian mission teacher in Liberia, William Wadé Harris, had a vision while in prison of the Angel Gabriel. Harris was there for his part in an attempted coup whose aim was to establish British rule in this one nominally independent part of West Africa. He had even raised the Union Jack near his home in Cape Palmas. The coup failed and Harris, who had long prided himself on being a civilized Christian Glebo, wearing western clothes and teaching western ideas, was now disillusioned and in prison, ripe for a religious conversion which made of him the most effective Christian evangelist Africa ever experienced. In a quite brief period of time between 1913 and 1915 he would convert tens of thousands of people in Ivory Coast, Gold Coast, and elsewhere from their traditional beliefs to a simple basic form of Christianity. Their conversion endured. The Angel Gabriel had ordered him both to burn the pagan 'fetishes' he had hitherto never given up and to abandon his western clothes, including his shoes, and wear instead a single piece of white cloth with a hole for his head. So dressed and armed with cross, Bible, and calabash, and accompanied by two wives, he became a prophet of Christ proclaiming God. The shoes had a special poignancy. The Episcopalian clergy were recognized to be the best-dressed body of coloured ministers in Liberia, and Harris had surely been anxious to fit that image. Almost the only thing we have written in his hand is an order in October 1907 for various items from an American catalogue, including a sewing machine and two pairs of 'men's stylish shoes'.[1] How much those shoes must have mattered to him. And how perceptive was the Angel Gabriel to insist that they above all must be abandoned. The prophet of Africa must walk free of all such westernisms. If one reads the remarkable study by James Krabill on the Christian hymns of the Dida,[2] one of the many groups converted by Harris in his great evangelistic tour, a group of people subsequently untouched for decades by any other outside evangelist, one can see how worthwhile Harris's sacrifice proved.

The story of Harris can be symbolic for the central thrust of twentieth-century Christian history, but only up to a point. The century began with a well-organized missionary offensive, Protestant and Catholic, on the non-western world, of a scale never before seen. We can observe it at its most public and thoughtful at the Edinburgh International Missionary Conference of 1910, out of which the organized Ecumenical Movement grew, or in the ever-expanding activities directed by the Roman Congregation of Propaganda Fide, or, again, in the activities of the Bible Societies and the multiplication of scriptural translations in more and more languages—probably the most culturally determinative and yet uncontrollable factor within the entire missionary movement. Translating the Bible not only made Christians, often of no hitherto known church, but also forged national identities. In theory all this remained a properly controlled enterprise in which non-western people were seen as above all receivers, only very slightly co-operators. Catechists and interpreters were seldom mentioned by name in missionary literature, prophets were looked on with alarm. Almost alone among mission theorists, Roland Allen argued for what one may call the Harris model.

Yet the mass conversion movement in Igboland, a thousand miles east of Harris's territory, largely into the Catholic Church, guided by the Irish missionary, Bishop Shanahan, looks remarkably similar. Here too 1913 was a crucial year: 'At last the era of Patrick is being realized in Igboland', Shanahan announced.[3] 'As we move from town to town, idols are toppling of their own accord and the cross of Christ is being erected in their place'—just as it was in the footsteps of Harris. It is true that here, unlike among the Dida, there was a modicum of European clerical control, but in essence the two 'expansions' were comparably 'spontaneous' to use Allen's preferred term.[4] They were replicated hundreds of times in Africa and elsewhere. In Asia one can think of the Naga and other peoples in India, the Batak in Sumatra, or the Toradjas of Central Sulawesi, the inhabitants of the Moluccas and, later, the peoples of South Korea. Some of these conversion movements go back well into the nineteenth century but it was in the course of the twentieth that the local churches deriving from them in literally thousands of places became stabilized and anxious to assert their own character and autonomy *vis-à-vis* the West. In Asia and Latin America they were joining an already quite sturdy Christian presence of several centuries, oldest in Kerala, but from the seventeenth century also in China, Japan, Vietnam, Sri Lanka, Flores, East Timor, as in Mexico, Peru, and Brazil.

While in most cases these communities had been in principle under the control of foreign clergy, the characteristic relationship had often been one of tension and a supposed impotence on the part of the non-European. It is true that the missionary input in the first half of the twentieth century, particularly on the Catholic side, was huge and much of it immensely impressive in terms of personal dedication and even language learning. Nevertheless, almost everywhere the main line of twentieth-century development lay across a growing anxiety on the part of non-western Christians to exist as churches, not missions. Only very exceptional missionaries like Vincent

Lebbe, C. F. Andrews, and David Paton showed any real sympathy with the need to emancipate Asian Christianity from its European shackles. Pius XI's personal consecration of the first six Chinese bishops in 1926 was one of the most significant visible steps in the huge shift of leadership which happened almost everywhere in the course of the century. The first Japanese Archbishop of Tokyo was appointed in 1936, the first African Catholic bishop of the Latin rite, Joseph Kiwanuka, in 1939. Once again, Kiwanuka's episcopal consecration in St Peter's, this time by Pius XII, was a clear enough indication of direction. Nevertheless the main churches, throughout the middle years of the century, held back from any full-scale implementation of such a policy. When Pius died in 1958 Kiwanuka had been joined by only ten other black diocesan bishops throughout the whole of Africa. It was the combined pressures of nationalism, Communism, and the termination of western empires, together with new theologies of mission and inculturation associated with the World Council of Churches and the Second Vatican Council, which really opened the gates to full public recognition of the churches of the South in the last third of the century.

China, the world's greatest nation, as well as Asia's, presents the most striking case of Christianity's twentieth-century, non-western, predicament. Its Christian history goes back many centuries, but the growth of its church has been affected, again and again, by western political and cultural intervention, an infamous combination of Opium Wars and the claim to be protectors of China's Christians, an immeasurable insult to her self-respect. By the inter-war years the struggle to free Chinese Christianity from missionary domination had cut deep into the church's soul. The endeavours of men like W. T. Wu and Lebbe to disentangle the one from the other were seen as a profound betrayal by 90 per cent of missionaries: 'I have heard again and again in Tianjin', wrote one Maryknoll missionary back to his Father General in America in August 1947, 'that the big danger to the Church in China is not the Communists but the native clergy.'[5] Whether, even in 1953, after the Communist conquest of China and expulsion of missionaries, many Christians in the west were willing to listen to David Paton's message in his striking afterword, *Christian Missions and the Judgement of God* (London, 1953), seems doubtful: 'The right word to describe what has happened to Christian missions in China is "debâcle" . . . The end of the missionary era was the will of God.'[6] A will brought about by Communism. How many western Christians could believe in that?

It proved, however, to be not only missionaries who were expected to disappear. Numerous Chinese Christians were glad to see the missionaries go, and thinkers with the stature of Y. T. Wu and T. C. Chao sought desperately to relate Christianity positively to the new Communist order, but their compliance would not be sufficient to spare the church. Death and rebirth had to go deeper than that. In a way, the intransigent Catholic Archbishop of Shanghai, Gong Pinmei, whose family had been Christian for centuries, represented his church best. Shanghai was the heartland of old Catholicism and Archbishop Gong could count on the loyalty of his people. He was tried in 1960 and sentenced to life imprisonment, to be replaced by someone more compliant. But in the Cultural Revolution of the following years every form of Christianity was expected to disappear. 'We had no church', one Christian later explained, 'but the church in our hearts.'[7] Observers in the west wrote Chinese Christianity off, yet today the churches in China, despite much continued government harassment, include millions of believers and appear to be rapidly expanding. The great Chinese persecution may prove in the end to be not so different in its effects from that of the persecution of Diocletian. Whether that is so or not, it will depend entirely on Chinese. What Communism did eliminate—to Christianity's actual benefit—was the missionary factor.

The Prophet Harris and his converts among the Ebrie and Dida at one end of the century, the Chinese Church by the 1990s at the other, do both, in their different ways, present the requirement of Christian growth to break out from the iron fist of western models. They remain relatively extreme examples but they stand for what is most important and central to twentieth-century Christian history worldwide: the turn to the south and the east, which is also, by and large, a turn from the affluent to the poor. The many hundreds of African and Asian bishops now ruling their own dioceses in the Catholic and Anglican communions, where at the start of the century there were none, are its most obvious witness. So are Religious Orders, fading away in Europe but growing almost as fast in Asia. Nowhere is the Society of Jesus expanding comparably to India, where again missionaries from the west are now few and far between. Most of the names of Christians internationally known in the latter part of the century are connected with places which were either ecclesiastically non-existent or very little regarded a hundred years ago: Helder Camara of Recife, Oscar Romero of San

Salvador, Desmond Tutu of Cape Town, Teresa of Calcutta. Despite the enthusiasm of the Edinburgh Conference in 1910 with its establishment backing reflected in telegrams from King George V, Theodore Roosevelt, and the German Colonial Office, no one could really have imagined at the time how huge or uncontrollable would be Christianity's expansion in unexpected places, making the whole southern half of Africa, for instance, substantially a Christian continent, or that ninety years later a growing flow of missionaries would be issuing forth from Kerala or South Korea, or that Igboland, still hardly started on its conversion in 1900, would be represented in Rome by a leading curial Cardinal long before the end of the century. Even less would anyone have foreseen how greatly this would affect the internal balance of Christianity.

That alteration in balance does, of course, also owe a great deal to what had been going on within the old heartlands of the churches, a series of contestations with forces both external and internal to Christianity, which have seen some remarkable victories and yet seem to have been left confused, unsure of the future, withdrawing from many of their traditional institutions, in deep numerical decline. Faced with three principal antagonists—Fascism, Communism, and agnostic humanism—the twentieth-century churches of Europe and North America put up a remarkable struggle. Fascism and Nazism were in part internal enemies, unlike Communism which was overwhelmingly external. The problem with the former was that they appealed to so many of the less happy traditions which had for long run rife within the life of the devout—nationalism, anti-Semitism, authoritarianism. Moreover the struggle with

Communism encouraged and seemingly excused a deeper complicity with Fascism—in Spain and elsewhere. It would then be a dangerous misreading to see the Christian struggle with these movements as one in which most Christians or church leaders saw the issues plain. They did not. It was a night battle. Even, for example, many members of the small minority of Protestants who belonged to the Confessing Church, basically an anti-Nazi protest movement, still sympathized with some of the nationalist aspects of what they were struggling against. Few indeed were those who saw things with the clarity of Dietrich Bonhoeffer. The same was true of most Catholics in Italy and many in France where the Pétainist appeal to Catholics was huge. It is impossible to claim with plausibility that Pius XII recognized how much was at stake in the struggle, but Bishop Headlam of Gloucester, formerly Regius Professor of Divinity in Oxford, proved at least as blind about the reality of Nazism.

Nevertheless, out of that maelstrom at the heart of the century grew a new Christianity. One sees some of its characteristics already in the discussions of the 1937 Oxford Conference of Life and Work, so meticulously prepared by Joe Oldham. One sees it in the writings of Jacques Maritain, one of the few Catholics to take a firm anti-Franco stand, or Christopher Dawson. The old political and even ecclesiastical shaping of the churches at the heart of Christendom altered decisively and irretrievably at that time. Catholicism accepted political democracy in a way it had never done hitherto. If its American wing had hitherto seemed almost deviant—under suspicion of the heresy of 'Americanism'—it now became normative. Protestants set up the World Council of Churches and Catholics soon found it impossible to remain aloof from the working, or even the ideas, of the Ecumenical Movement. In many ways the most characteristic viewpoints of the Second Vatican Council already took shape in the later 1930s in the minds of men like Chenu, Congar, and de Lubac, friends and allies of Maritain, much as their *Nouvelle Théologie* was under suspicion in the post-war period. The fathers of the Ecumenical Movement were, it may be admitted, struggling manfully with rather inadequate tools but they re-established a sense of Christian, rather than denominational, belonging in a way that has proved decisive. Their favoured model of unity, culled from the Church of South India and exported to the World Council especially by Lesslie Newbigin, Bishop of Madurai, was too simple to work, canonized as it was at the Third Assembly at New Delhi in 1961, but, even here, the impact of the South on wider thinking is worthy of note. The World Council itself, established so convincingly by the most outstanding leaders of the mid-century, with a great post-war flourish at Amsterdam in 1948, seemed to be becoming a new central pillar to the Christian world, and Wim Visser't Hooft, its first General Secretary, a Dutch Barthian, was without doubt one of the most significant religious figures of our century. All this grew out of the mid-century crisis, centred on the Second World War. It is true that the significance of Visser't Hooft's office has paled astonishingly fast. The attempt, deliberate or not, to make of Geneva an alternative centre of Christendom to Rome and a more embracing one does not appear to have worked. The World Council may be fading in significance while Rome seems more central than ever. The centrality of the papacy, no matter what one thinks of its policies, has grown and grown. And yet even that could not have been the case if the Ecumenical Movement had not prepared the ground for it. Without Visser't Hooft and all that he signified, one could hardly imagine Archbishop Carey and the Metropolitan Athanasios standing beside Pope John Paul II to push open the Jubilee Door of St Paul's basilica in Rome.

But without Christianity's second and most striking twentieth-century antagonist, Communism, it is unlikely that a Polish pope would have been the man they were assisting. Christian life has been permeated with a sense of struggle with Communism through most of the century. Despite valorous attempts of a handful of Christians to belong to both sides in this war, the lines have been drawn pretty clearly, ever since the early Leninist onslaught on the Orthodox Church in Russia. The roll call of martyrs has been a long one. Almost no one at the time of the Yalta Agreement in 1945, in which Churchill and Roosevelt handed over to Stalin's control most of eastern Europe, or during the long years of religious persecution which followed, could have imagined that forty-five years after Yalta Communism would explode into dissolution, torn apart by intellectual aridity and practical incapacity, and that the churches, who were the only public institutions which in any way managed to stand up to it, would appear to have triumphed. Polish Catholicism proved tougher than Soviet Communism. John Paul II symbolized that stupendous victory but so did the subsequent rebuilding of a huge cathedral in Moscow torn down on Stalin's orders. Yet it is easier to struggle than to win and part of the seeming vacuity of late twentieth-century western Christianity derives precisely from the loss of an enemy. Victory can be more destructive of morale than the long haul of a war which seems to have no end. Polish Catholics in particular now hardly know which way to turn. A rather arid and triumphalistic restorationism easily fills the gap.

Vastly more difficult has it proved for twentieth-century Christianity to face its third rival: liberal, capitalist, scientific humanism. Indeed, it could seem as if the churches themselves had been but the Trojan Horse enabling their most subtle enemy to take possession of their dearest heartlands. For here again Christianity has had to struggle with something within it as much as without, and it has unquestionably not been so successful in doing so. The entire history of post-Enlightenment theology in the west could be read as a herculean struggle to retain credibility for faith in a culture where the rational, the scientific, and the materialist have been claiming an ever more total authority over the interpretation of reality and yet where the movement of mind represented in these terms derived, in part, from one thread within Christianity, however much the churches came to fear and endeavour to rebut it. The massive decline of Christian influence within European society in this period is not, then, due simply to an alien attacking from without but at least as much to a formation of mind fostered by Christianity and with many friends within its walls. The theological struggle nevertheless necessitated by this predicament of Christian faith facing modernity has, indeed, been prodigious. If one considers the theologians, philosophers, and historians who have been most influential within this struggle in the course of the twentieth century, such as Barth, Bultmann, Tillich, Bonhoeffer, the

Niebuhrs, Maritain, Teilhard de Chardin, Rahner, Congar, von Balthasar, Pannenberg, one may conclude that the twentieth century has been one of four peak periods in post-apostolic theological thinking, the others being the later fourth and early fifth century, the thirteenth, and the sixteenth. In each case the main age of creativity lasted less than a hundred years, each time establishing a new pattern to the Christian mind. The freedom, diversity, and creativity of this latest period of thought has been remarkable. Nevertheless, the foundations have been shaken—the foundations of every side of Christian belief. Moreover, this has been in response to, and as a consequence of, the still wider social and intellectual shaking of the structures of western Christianity. Thus, for centuries a lay–clerical divide, a male–female divide, and a series of denominational divisions have been decisive in shaping the public life and organization of Christianity. All these have largely collapsed.

Take one little example. In 1899 a Baptist minister in South London, F. B. Meyer, wrote to ask the Anglican Bishop of Southwark, Edward Talbot, a man of intelligence and moral stature who had previously been Warden of Keble College, if he could possibly attend the centenary celebration of the Baptist Sunday School Society, which catered for four thousand Southwark children. 'Would it be quite impossible for you to look in?', Meyer pleaded. 'It would be a noble act of catholicity.'[8] Talbot replied that it was quite impossible. It was 'a matter of clear principle'. To show the slightest recognition of any good that the Baptist Sunday Schools were doing would be to countenance 'the breach of unity which is so colossal an evil'. By the end of the century Meyer's view of catholicity had prevailed, daringly marginal as it had seemed in his time, while Talbot's response can only raise a laugh. What has triumphed is a sense of spiritual communion embracing all the main traditions. No less striking has been the collapse of the still older ecclesiastical division between men and women, with the exclusion of the latter from sacramental and preaching activity, other than the act of baptizing in cases of emergency. We are still struggling with the breaking down of this most formidable middle wall but essentially it seems to have gone, even if the pope would not agree. While we doubtless have still a long way to go, Christianity at the end of the twentieth century was already experiencing a scale of feminine ministry, theology, and general initiative unparalleled in any other century. The theological shaking of the foundations has thus been taking place within a far wider ecclesiastical revolution which has done much to sweep away the structures the churches of the west inherited from late classical times, the Middle Ages, and the Reformation era.

In assessing the success of the twentieth-century theological movement in rethinking Christian faith in the context of modernity, one may judge that it had passed its peak by the 1970s while the general western erosion of Christianity was, on the contrary, progressing ever faster; against that one may argue that what most damaged the middle of the century theological renaissance was still its division between Protestant, Catholic, and Orthodox segments, a division subsequently overcome. While the most powerful minds were within the Protestant segment, their achievement was gravely impaired by the extent to which they remained cut off from the central Catholic tradition. Change here came with the

Second Vatican Council and its aftermath, when the peak of Protestant theologizing was past. Institutionally, the effects of conciliar *aggiornamento* remain confused and hard to evaluate; but intellectually that is much less the case. Probably the most remarkable development in the west in the last thirty years of the century has been a fusion of Catholic and Protestant thinking, coupled with an increased infusion of Orthodox influence. The strength of Christian theology at the close of the century lay not in great names. In this it could not compete with an earlier generation. It lay in the ability to draw together the biblical, patristic, medieval scholastic, Reformation, and post-Enlightenment inheritance within a single functional enterprise. Essentially this means that the Ecumenical Movement, which was so central to the history of Christianity throughout the century, has succeeded intellectually, even if it has not succeeded institutionally. How much difference this will make to the long-term intellectual standing of Christianity *vis-à-vis* the wider society, it remains impossible to say. Only a very rash person would endeavour to foretell the intellectual shape of the twenty-first century.

The twentieth was a century of great theologians, of remarkably forceful popes, and of numerous martyrs from Chalmers in its opening year to Pavel Florensky, Miguel Pro, Edith Stein, Franz Jägerstätter, and Oscar Romero. Whatever faults twentieth-century Christianity as a whole may be accused of, anaemia is not one.

But if this was a century of martyrs, it was also one of quite this-worldly spirituality, and indeed it was often the this-worldliness which led to martyrdom. Of that combination Bonhoeffer was prototypical—the man who could write 'Is it not true to say that individualistic concern for personal salvation has almost left us all?'[9] and yet who could also say, immediately before execution, 'This is for me the beginning.' A question remains whether the turn to a this-worldly spirituality does not necessarily bring with it a disintegrating secularization, evident not in the heroic figure of the martyr but in the community at large. That turn was most evident in the 1960s, when the this-worldly fervour of Vatican II and the WCC at Uppsala could be matched by the start of a quantitative nose-dive in western Christianity. If the strategies of both the Rome of John Paul II and Pentecostal Evangelicalism have favoured of late a less secular rhetoric, are they that much more in tune with what we can call 'Southern Hemisphere Christianity'?

This brings me to attempt an overall characterization of our difficult century. When I have pondered the character of its Christian history as a whole and asked myself with what it might most helpfully be compared, I have thought of the seventh to ninth centuries. Surprising as it may seem, the two periods have much in common. At that time the heartlands of Christianity were still undoubtedly in the Greek east. So much so that the Latin west accepted unquestioningly the ecumen-icity of the Council of Chalcedon in 680, Nicaea in 787, and Constantinople in 869. All three included papal representation but western participation was otherwise minimal and the gap between east and west already immense. But the real vitality of the church, the main growth area, was by then far away to the north-west in the seemingly uncivilized areas of England, northern France, Holland, and Germany. When the Greek monk Theodore laid down the basic lines of the church in

England in the late seventh century or Boniface did so in Germany in the eighth, few people in Constantinople will have taken the news very seriously. Yet in point of fact the whole shape of the Christian world was undergoing a sea change and the places which would soon matter most were Paris, Canterbury, Cologne, and the like. For a thousand years they remained so. Only in the twentieth century may this have changed decisively with western Europe retaining, as Byzantium long retained, a sort of primacy of prestige but in fact giving way to younger, more dynamic, perhaps also more simplistic, churches. Just as Russia would renew the Byzantine tradition yet change it greatly too, so has North America taken over much of the mantle of northern Europe while privatizing its inheritance. But what matters even more is the emergence into full vitality of still larger churches in the southern continents of Latin America, Africa, and Asia. Upon them may the future third millennium of Christianity depend, just as at the start of the second millennium it had come to depend on the young churches of north-west Europe.

There remains a profound effort to control the global expansion of Christianity, an effort derived chiefly from two sides: on the one part the Roman Curia, on the other American fundamentalist and Pentecostal Protestantism. If the growth in prestige and authority of the papacy throughout the century has been remarkable, hardly less so has been the growth of the Pentecostal movement, generally dated as beginning in its modern form with the Azusa Street Revival in Los Angeles in 1906. As this has spread, so has it diversified, first between black and white forms, but then into a varying mix stressing miracles, speaking in tongues, eschatological expectation, the prosperity gospel often linked with tele-evangelism and an extreme form of biblical fundamentalism. In some countries it is now hardly separable from evangelicalism. It spread, too, from distinct Pentecostal churches into the mainline traditions, including Catholicism and Anglicanism, with a redefinition as the Charismatic Movement from the 1960s. Its impact on the vitality and diversity of worship is well-nigh universal. What was initially very much a North American movement has become a worldwide one, particularly influential in Latin America, Indonesia, and parts of Africa. It is a matter of academic dispute how far in its global form it remains American-inspired and controlled. The flow of literature, money, and personnel out of the United States along Pentecostal lines is not disputable, but it remains open to question who is using whom and how far Pentecostalism elsewhere is essentially local in its inspiration, however much willing to make use of American props. At least some of its attraction must derive from its origins within black American culture. Internally to Christianity the struggle between these two models—a Rome-centred institutionalized and clerically-controlled Catholicism and a more apparently flexible Pentecostalist North American-inspired Protestantism—has probably been the most significant feature of late twentieth-century history, a struggle played out above all in Latin America, hitherto almost a Catholic preserve. At times as in Guatemala the intrusion of Pentecostalism has been as bloody and as politically-linked as anything in Catholic South American history, a counter to the social conversion of Catholicism symbolized by Liberation Theology and Base Communities. Whether either the Vatican or North American

Pentecostalism will be very successful in the long run in controlling the Christianity of the southern hemisphere remains uncertain. Moreover if, on one flank, Rome in the post-Communist age has been fighting Pentecostal inroads, on another its target has been liberalism and in the latter struggle it has actually found an ally in Pentecostal Evangelicals.

For the rest of us control is no longer possible but the handing on of an intellectual and spiritual heritage can still matter a lot. In the eighth century John Damascene, working under Muslim Caliphs in the Middle East in a church no longer both privileged and constrained by the power of the emperor in Constantinople, was able to put together a rather free, mature, well-rounded summary of the Greek theology of earlier centuries to offer to the future. Something similar could prove to have been the role of western theology in the twentieth century. It ceased to be in thrall to the nationalism and imperialism of the great European powers, the privileges of a centuries-long Babylonian Captivity. The very dissolution of the traditional Christendom character of Europe may have enabled its modern believers to experience a mature intellectual freedom which could not save their churches from further decline but which did make it possible for them to offer the future heartlands of Christianity a theology immeasurably much richer and more faithful to the tradition than was available at the start of the century. If that is true, then the very decline of the west has had its own fruitfulness, just another example of the law within Christianity's long history that the increase of the new is dependent on the decrease of the old.

10

PROSPECT

Richard Harries

During the 1960s sociologists of religion suggested that the world was experiencing an irreversible process of secularization. Then sharper questions began to be asked about the criteria which were being used. At one time it was reported that there were 40,000 professional fortune tellers in France, a greater number than there were priests, and that some of these were being employed by companies when making business decisions. This fact, which is reflected in the vast numbers of people who read their horoscope, may indicate a number of things, but it is hardly the mark of a secular society. One phenomenon which the early exponents of secularization could not account for was the United States of America. This was and is at once the most modern society in the world and one of the most religious.

At the beginning of the third millennium sociologists of religion now see the world rather differently. In some respects it seems that the more modern a society becomes, the more religion becomes prominent. Industrialization and globalization, far from leading to the withering away of religion, have heightened its importance. Indonesia is a striking example. Indonesia is at once the most populous Muslim state in the world and for long was the most tolerant. However, modernization has brought people into the cities from the islands and rural areas. Whereas in the past people found their identity as part of a settled village community, in the displacement of a modern city their identity has been built up round the mosque or the church. Unfortunately this heightened role of religious communities has been exploited by unscrupulous political forces in the Moluccas and elsewhere.

In other countries religion has become more prominent not just in terms of local communities but nationally, because it has become bound up with national identity as in, for example, Malaysia with Islam and India through the strongly Hindu BJP Party. As Christianity faces the future two seemingly contradictory phenomena confront it. One is the revival of non-Christian religions and the other is what sociologists have termed 'European Exceptionalism', the fact that Europe seems steadfastly resistant to what has been happening elsewhere. In contrast to much of the rest of the world institutional religion has become less significant as a public player.

Adrian Hastings showed how the twentieth century was one of the great missionary periods of the church, with the Christian faith taking hold in almost every country in the world. He also showed how it had shed its Western trappings and emerged with indigenous leadership. At the same time, at least since World War II, the other major religions in the world have been gathering strength. Islam, which earlier in the twentieth century had been written off as dormant or decadent, became, for a variety of reasons, economic, social, political, and religious, a force to be reckoned with in many countries. The vast majority of Muslims, like the vast majority of Christians, are moderate, decent people, who seek to practise their religion in peace. Nevertheless, in Indonesia, the Sudan, Pakistan, and Nigeria there have been bitter clashes between Muslims and Christians. In India more than a hundred Christians have been killed in recent years by Hindu nationalists. So considered on a world-wide scale, the fundamental fact about the future of Christianity is the resurgence and strength of the world's major religions to which the churches have to relate. There is the pressing social and political task of living peacefully together. There is also the theological task of relating Christian faith to other views of the world that have their own integrity and vitality. This theological task is being perceived very differently by European and North American theologians on the one hand, and on the other, those Christians living in countries where there are religious tensions.

In the western world a lively debate continues to take place between those who believe that the truth of God is given exclusively in Christianity, those who take a pluralist view, arguing that all religions are but dim apprehensions of one not fully known truth, and those who believe that the faith of Christ can be discerned in all religions and it is the role of Christianity to recognize this and bring it to fulfilment. There is no consensus on this issue and the debate continues. Meanwhile the way of dialogue seems both more practical and requires less theological superstructure. The 1988 Lambeth Conference for Anglican bishops round the world suggested that dialogue had three aspects. First, trying to understand the dialogue partner in their own terms, avoiding stereotypes and letting them speak for themselves. Secondly, exploring the possibility of common ground, and thirdly, recognizing the real differences. For genuine dialogue involves bringing those differences into the relationship. There can be no universally agreed goal for interfaith dialogue. To suggest such would fall into the same error as pluralism, positing a bird's eye view above the traditions in which religious claims are made. We do not have such a vantage point. Nevertheless, Christians can have a goal for their dialogue with other religions. The goal may perhaps be seen in terms of analogies to the reconstitution of society round Jesus Christ (the Kingdom of God as made present through him). Discovering these analogies can lead Christians to live more seriously before the truths of their own faith. As Rowan Williams has written: 'Can we so *rediscover* our own foundational story in the acts and hopes of others that we ourselves are re-converted and are also able to bring those acts and hopes in relation with Christ for their fulfilment by the re-creating grace of God.'[1] This emphasis upon reconverting themselves brings out a crucial aspect of the relationships between religions for the future. There is a necessity for them to be self-critical in the light of their own core beliefs. Without slipping into relativism the challenge facing all religions is whether they can shift from their traditional stance of aggressive superiority to other religions to one of penitent and grateful living out of their own truths, enlarging those truths through contact with partners in dialogue.

Outside the developed world dialogue, in one form or another, is a matter of life and death. In some places there is active proselytizing and in others the attempt to impose religious law on a country as a whole. In such circumstances dialogue is not a luxury but a necessity for living peacefully together. The accusation is often made that religion either causes or exacerbates conflict. It is certainly true that when a larger political grouping breaks up, as did the Soviet Union and the former Yugoslavia, religion can become a marker of identity in the ensuing ethnic conflicts. Conflict is endemic to human life and the resurgence of religion on the world stage means that it will continue to be a marker of identity. There is clearly a major responsibility on religious leaders to draw on the resources of their respective religions that make for peaceful co-existence.

The United States remains the most modern and powerful country in the world. Its people also have an extraordinary capacity to believe. Of Americans, whether or not they are Christians, 84 per cent believe that God performs miracles and 48 per cent say that they have personally experienced or witnessed an event which they consider to have been miraculous. Amongst Evangelical Protestants the figure is 71 per cent. Europeans are much more sceptical. Nevertheless, at the beginning of the third millennium an interesting phenomenon is emerging. In the UK for example, in December 1999, Opinion Research Business Poll showed that 27 per cent of the population claim to be 'spiritual', the same percentage as claim to be religious. What is perhaps even more significant is that whereas 39 per cent of the population described themselves as not religious, only 12 per cent confessed to being 'not a spiritual person'. In other words, 88 per cent of the population resist being described as non-spiritual.

The same trend was underscored by the recent opinion poll commissioned in connection with the BBC's series *Soul of Britain*. Well over 50 per cent of the population, for example, believe in the soul. The challenge facing the churches in Europe is whether they can draw on the resources of Christian truth and communicate it in such a way that will resonate with this growing category of self-defined spiritual persons.

Within the wider question about the relationship between Christianity and other faiths, there is the special, unique relationship between Christianity and Judaism. During the closing decades of the twentieth century scholars became more aware of the appalling record of the churches towards Judaism, the long history of 'the teaching of contempt' as well as the active harassment and persecution. All this helped to prepare the ground for secular anti-Semitism and the unspeakable horrors of the Holocaust. It was the publication of *Nostra Aetate* by the Second Vatican Council in 1965 that marked the beginning of a revolution in Christian attitudes to Judaism. Affirming a common 'spiritual patrimony' the Vatican Council said that the passion of Christ 'cannot be charged against all the Jews' and 'concerns the Church as such'. The Vatican followed this up with its *Guidelines* in 1975 and its *Notes for Preaching and Catechesis* in 1985. There are now innumerable documents from the Protestant churches calling for a fundamental re-appraisal of Christianity's relationship with Judaism. There are, however, many unresolved questions and, more important, the fundamental re-appraisal, affecting biblical interpretation, preaching, and liturgy, has not yet begun to really affect the life of the church as a whole, particularly the Protestant churches, in the way it should. Too often still Judaism is simply set up as a foil for Christian teaching. The work of educating the Christian public into a proper understanding of Judaism needs to be done afresh in every generation.

Consideration of the Holocaust has not only called into question Christianity's whole relationship with Judaism but poses the question about what, if any, theology can be done after it. Tears, anger, and silence seem the only possible moral response. But it is not only the Holocaust. Modern communications mean that every day we are battered with stories of murder, cruelty, and suffering. Although the twentieth century in the end rejected both Marxism and a fundamentalist Freudianism, both those philosophies ate into the European soul, so that the novelist Iris Murdoch could write 'All that consoles is fake'. So the Christianity of the future has to face not simply philosophical questions, but a moral critique and a continuing question mark about how it can convey a message of hope that does not seem a cheap evasion of the continuing human tragedy. Its hope must be that it lives, and can only live, in the power of the crucified one.

Cheap and easy religion will always have a future. When it is allied to a nationalism or other political causes, it will be an ugly one. But there are those who are faithful, in all parts of the world, and their witness will prevail. In Europe, despite the continuous disparagement of religion from the national print media, the arts continue to have a fruitful relationship with the Christian faith. It is not just the continuing popularity of classical works with explicitly Christian themes, it is that much modern work has Christian resonances, whether the producer of the work is or is not a Christian believer themselves. In music especially, but also poetry, if to a lesser extent in the visual arts and the theatre, there is that which keeps open the possibility of a luminous enchantment even for the cultured despisers of our age. The astonishing success of the exhibition of Christian art at the National Gallery 'Seeing Salvation' indicates the continuing capacity of Christian scenes and images to resonate with a wider public.

The history of Christianity over the last 2,000 years brings home the fact that the truth of the church's message cannot be measured in terms of its territorial advancement. Once, Christian North Africa was a glory of the church. At times Jerusalem has been a Christian city. In 1453, after nearly 1,200 years, the most glittering Christian civilization the world has known fell. From the seventh century onwards Christianity gradually took hold in Europe and as European power grew so did Christian power and influence. With the rise of American power Christianity seemed even more in the ascendant. But now the mainstream denominations are in decline, even if not so steeply as in Europe. Evangelical Christianity remains strong, as does Pentecostalism in Latin America and both are vigorous in other parts of the world, not least in Africa. It is now said for example that there are more Anglicans in Nigeria alone than in the whole of the Church of England and the Episcopal Church of the United States of America. The Roman Catholic Church is particularly blessed by the strength of its universal dimension. For although vocations to the priesthood are nothing short of catastrophic in the United States and Europe, in India, for example, there are a growing number of people joining the religious orders. It is probably foolish to speculate about where the centre of gravity of Christianity will move next, though China presents an intriguing possibility with its vigorous underground congregations as well as the officially recognized ones. But whether there is gain or loss, advancement or retrenchment, always there is the hope that to do justice and love mercy is not in vain.

Notes

Notes to Chapter 1

1. 'Seneca saepe noster', Tertullian, *De Anima* 20.
2. A. Bonhoeffer, *Epiktet und das Neue Testament* (Giessen, 1911).
3. *Confessions* 6.16.26. Naturally Augustine also thought Epicurus wrong on important points (6.11.19) such as his denial of providential care (*contra Faustum* 20.10), belief in innumerable worlds (*City of God* 11.5), his incomprehension of Archimedes (*Util. Credendi* 6, 13). But he saw correctly that infants survive because they go for what is pleasant and avoid what is painful.
4. This claim became more strident in late antiquity as the barbarian threat became stronger.
5. So a rabbinic text in Strack-Billerbeck, *Kommentar z. NT aus Talmud und Midrasch* IV 2 (1928), 1203. The rabbi was unimpressed.
6. Mark 13: 14; 2 Thessalonians 2: 4.
7. John 11: 50.
8. The pagan Celsus, in Origen (*contra Celsum* 8.71), thought this a ludicrous dream. Justin Martyr came close to this aspiration.
9. Tertullian, *Apol.* 21.24.
10. Tertullian, *Apol.* 50.13.
11. *stasis*: Celsus in Origen 5.33.
12. Marcus Aurelius 11.3.
13. Porphyry, *De abstinentia* 2.37; cf. Augustine, *City of God* 2.24.
14. *Apol.* 39.7.
15. Eusebius, *HE* 8.1.2.
16. Ambrose, *Ep.* 15.3; Libanius, *Orat.* 45.27. It is illuminating that the gods were believed to be offended if criminals were executed at their feasts: Augustine, *City of God* 4.26. Most early Christian writers were against capital punishment and torture. Ambrose of Milan excommunicated Gallic bishops who had been a party to the prosecution and execution of Priscillian of Avila and his friends under the emperor Magnus Maximus.
17. Celsus in Origen 5.25.19.

18. Ammianus Marcellinus 28.4.24.

19. *Paganismus* occurs in Augustine, *Div. Qu. LXXXIII* 83.

20. 'What you call Sunday, we call the Lord's day (dominica)': Augustine, *contra Faustum* 18.5.

21. Augustine, *Sermo 178.4.*

22. Hippolytus, *Apost. Trad.* 26.8.

23. London Papyrus, 1914.28, edited by H. I. Bell, *Jews and Christians in Egypt* (1924).

24. Augustine, *Sermo Frangipane* 2.4 (p. 193, ed. Morin).

25. Galatians 3: 24.

26. Scholarios IV. 511.

27. *Tract. in ev. Joh.* 51.

28. Romans 2.

29. 1 Corinthians 7. Some of the language of this chapter has remarkable affinities with the second-century Stoic Epictetus.

30. Origen once observes that bishops of large cities, pampered by ladies of wealth and refinement, are unwilling to speak with ascetics on equal terms: *in Matt.* 16. 8.

31. Vigilantius, against whom Jerome wrote severely, provides some of the evidence for this.

32. Gregory of Tours, *Historia* 1.44.

33. Siricius, *ep.* 10.5, PL 20.1184.

34. Augustine, *De opere monachorum* 25, on economic motives. The Greek Life of Pachomius (ed. Halkin, Brussels, 1932) is also illuminating.

35. Augustine, *De bono conjugali* 29–30.

36. Augustine, *Contra ii epp. Pelag.* 2.11.

37. See the Pachomian *Praecepta* 127 f.

38. Augustine, *Sermo* 159.5. John Chrysostom has several references to this fact, e.g. *in Matt* 5.6; *in 1 Cor.* 20.5; *in Heb.* 11.3. Cf. Libanius, *orat.* 25.37 (free manual workers have to toil night and day to avert starvation). Cf. *Reallexikon für Antike und Christentum* XVI 688.

39. Homily on Ecclesiastes 4, PG. 36.663–8 = Gregory of Nyssa, *Opera* (Leiden, 1960 ff.) 5, 334–53.

40. Clement of Alexandria, *Stromateis* VI 71.

41. *Ep.* 222.2. In Augustine and other Western writers of his time 'dogmas' are something that heretics have.

42. See a classic account in D. J. Chitty, *The Desert a City* (Oxford, Blackwell 1966).
43. Ambrose, *De obitu Theodosii* 28; Augustine, *City of God* 5.26.

NOTES TO CHAPTER 2

1. Letter of Constantine to the *vicarius* of the province of North Africa, Spring, AD 314, preserved by Optatus, *Against the Donatists*, Appendix III.
2. Eusebius, *Vita Constantini* III.15.
3. Eusebius, *Tricennalian Oration*, trans. H. A. Drake, *In Praise of Constantine* (Berkeley and Los Angeles, 1976).
4. Trans. J. Wilkinson, *Egeria's Travels*, 3rd edn. (Warminster, 1999).
5. Trans. Robert C. Gregg, *Athanasius. The Life of Antony and the Letter to Marcellinus* (New York, 1980).
6. Trans. Richard Price, *A History of the Monks of Syria* (Kalamazoo, 1985).
7. Augustine, *Confessions* VIII.6.15.
8. Socrates, *Ecclesiastical History* VII.32.

NOTES TO CHAPTER 3

1. *Letters of Gregory the Great*, ix, 26.
2. Patrick Wormald, 'Bede, Beowulf and the Conversion of the Anglo-Saxon Aristocracy', in *Bede and Anglo-Saxon England*, ed. Robert T. Farrell, *British Archaeological Reports* 46 (Oxford, 1978).
3. Smaragdus of Verdun, *Via Regia*, chapter 16, *PL* 102, cols. 956–7.
4. In black and white in Henry Mayr-Harting, *Ottonian Book Illumination* (London, 1991), i, 58–9.
5. *St Gregory the Great, Pastoral Care (Regula Pastoralis)* translated by Henry Davis, Ancient Christian Writers no. 11 (New York, 1950).
6. *Bede, Ecclesiastical History of the English People,* iii, 3 and iii, 14 (Penguin Classics, Harmondsworth, 1968).
7. *Einhard, the Life of Charlemagne*, c. 22, in *Two Lives of Charlemagne* (Penguin Classics, Harmondsworth, 1969) 77.
8. Translated in P. D. King, *Charlemagne: Translated Sources* (Lambrigg, 1987), 309–10.

9. Translated in C. H. Talbot, *The Anglo-Saxon Missionaries in Germany* (London, 1954), pp. 75–8. Adrian Hastings, in his contribution to this volume, has not unreasonably seen the activities of St Boniface as where a new centre of things in Christian development lay in his time. I tried to do more justice to St Boniface than I can do here in *The Oxford Illustrated History of Christianity*, ed. John McManners (Oxford, 1990), 94–7, and in my *Coming of Christianity to Anglo-Saxon England* (3rd edn. London, 1991), 262–73.

10. King, *Charlemagne*, 229.

11. Katherine F. Drew, *The Lombard Laws* (University of Pennsylvania Press, 1973), 62.

12. The *Admonitio Generalis* (789) is translated in P. D. King, 209–20, and for a wholly reliable identification of scriptural citations one must go to the Latin text in *Monumenta Germaniae Historica: Capitularia* i ed. A. Boretius (Hanover, 1881), 58–60.

13. *Praeloquia* iii, 9, Migne's *Patrologia Latina* 136, col. 224C.

14. *Letters of Gregory the Great*, v, 44.

15. Quoted in Henry G. J. Beck, *The Pastoral Care of Souls in South-East France during the Sixth Century* (Rome, 1950), p. 267, note 42.

16. Thietmar of Merseburg, *Chronicon* (Berlin, 1995), i, c. 15 (ed. R. Holtzmann, p. 34), and vi, c. 64, p. 354.

17. Life of Burchard of Worms, cc. 3–4. MGH SS IV, 833–4.

18. Thietmar of Merseburg iv, c. 18, p. 152; iv, c. 26, p. 162.

19. Thietmar of Merseburg, ii, c. 21, p. 62.

20. Thietmar of Merseburg, ii, c. 27, p. 72.

21. The book is now in the Bayerische Staatsbibliothek, Munich, Clm 30111, fos. 33v-34r.

NOTES TO CHAPTER 4

1. I read this story as a child, but I cannot now remember where.

2. Cyril of Alexandria, *Third Letter to Nestorius* 12: ed. Lionel R. Wickham, *Cyril of Alexandria: Select Letters* (Oxford: Clarendon Press, 1983), 28.

3. John Stewart, *Nestorian Missionary Enterprise: The Story of a Church on Fire* (Edinburgh: T. & T. Clark, 1928).

4. J. F. Coakley, *The Church of the East and the Church of England. A History of the Archbishop of Canterbury's Assyrian Mission* (Oxford: Clarendon Press, 1992).

5. Compare T. S. Eliot, 'Little Gidding', § III, *The Four Quartets* (London: Faber, 1944), 41.

6. *Isaac of Nineveh (Isaac the Syrian), 'The Second Part', Chapters IV–XLI,* tr. Sebastian Brock, Corpus Scriptorum Christianorum Orientalium 555, Scriptores Syri 225 (Louvain: Peeters, 1995), *Homily* 39:6, 15 (pp. 165, 170).

7. *The Ascetical Homilies of Saint Isaac the Syrian,* [tr. Dana Miller] (Boston, MA: Holy Transfiguration Monastery, 1984), *Homily* 48 (p. 230). Compare *Mystic Treatises by Isaac of Nineveh,* tr. A. J. Wensinck (Amsterdam: Koninklijke Akademie van Wetenschappen, 1923), *Homily* 45 (p. 216).

8. *To Thalassius* 60, ed. C. Laga and C. Steel, Corpus Christianorum, Series Graeca 22 (Leuven: Brepols, 1990), 75.

9. *Disputed Questions (Ambigua)* 7 (*Patrologia Graeca* 91:1084CD); *On the Lord's Prayer,* ed. P. van Deun, Corpus Christianorum, Series Graeca 23 (Leuven: Brepols, 1991), 50.

10. This comes from the abstract of a lecture given by Fr Gervase in 1945: see *Eastern Churches Quarterly* 6:5 (1946), 227; reprinted in *Eastern Churches Review* 4:2 (1972), 118.

11. See his seminal study 'Neuf cent ans après: Notes sur le "Schisme oriental"', in *1054–1954: L'Eglise et les Eglises, Etudes et Travaux sur l'Unité chrétienne offerts à Dom Lambert Beauduin,* Collection Irénikon, vol. 1 (Gembloux: Chevetogne, 1954), especially 80–87.

12. *The Eastern Schism* (Oxford: Clarendon Press, 1955), 151.

13. J. Besson, *La Syrie sainte* (Paris, 1660), p. 11; compare Timothy Ware, *Eustratios Argenti: A Study of the Greek Church under Turkish Rule* (Oxford: Clarendon Press, 1964), 16–41.

14. Quoted in Joseph Gill, *The Council of Florence* (Cambridge: University Press, 1959), 163.

15. Quoted in Joseph Gill, *Personalities of the Council of Florence and Other Essays* (Oxford: Basil Blackwell, 1964), 267. Later on, as the Council drew towards its close, Bessarion acceded to the Roman Catholic standpoint, but here he expresses a typically Byzantine view.

16. *Peri tis Archis tou Papa Antirrisis* (Iassy, 1682), 195.

17. In Serge A. Zenkovsky (ed.), *Medieval Russia's Epics, Chronicles, and Tales* (revised edn., New York: Meridian Books, 1974), 97.

18. See his article 'A Dark Age Crisis: Aspects of the Iconoclastic

Controversy', in *English Historical Review* 88 (1973), 1–34; reprinted in *Society and the Holy in Late Antiquity* (London: Faber, 1982), 251–301.

19. Iconoclasm and the Monophysites', in Anthony Bryer and Judith Herrin (eds.), *Iconoclasm* (Birmingham: Centre for Byzantine Studies, 1977), 57.

20. In more recent Orthodox observance, icons are usually blessed with special prayers; but this was not as yet the practice in the eighth or ninth century.

21. *On the holy icons* 1:16, 21: ed. Bonifatius Kotter, *Die Schriften des Johannes von Damaskos*, vol. 3, Patristische Texte und Studien 17 (Berlin/New York: Walter de Gruyter, 1975), 89–90, 109.

22. A hesychast is one who seeks *hesychia*, inner stillness or silence of the heart, through the practice of contemplative prayer.

23. *On commandments and doctrines* 113; in G. E. H. Palmer, Philip Sherrard and Kallistos Ware (eds.), *The Philokalia*, vol. 4 (London: Faber, 1995), 237.

24. *The Life in Christ* 4; tr. C. J. deCatanzaro (Crestwood, NY: St Vladimir's Seminary Press, 1974), 123–4, 148.

NOTES TO CHAPTER 5

1. The full title of this lecture, as of all modern writings mentioned by name in this chapter, is given in Further Reading on pp. 258–9.

2. A bibliography of Beryl Smalley's writings is appended to the volume of her collected essays entitled *Studies in Medieval Thought and Learning from Abelard to Wyclif* (London, 1981), 417–22.

3. *Registrum Gregorii VII*, bk 3, no. 21; ed. E. Caspar, *Das Register Gregors VII*. Monumenta Germaniae Historica, Epistolae selectae [separatim editae], vol. 2 (Berlin, 1955), p. 288, lines 11–14,

4. *Registrum*, bk 1, no. 49; ed. Caspar, 75.14–19.

5. M. Maccarrone, *Studi su Innocenzo III*. Italia Sacra. Studi et documenti de storia ecclesiastica, vol. 17 (Padua, 1972), 341–431. Manuscripts: 425–31.

6. J. Alberigo and others (eds.), *Conciliorum oecumenicorum decreta*, 3rd edn. (Bologna, 1973), p. 239, lines 25–6. A translation of the decrees of the fourth Lateran council is available in H. Rothwell (ed.), *English Historical Documents, 1189–1327* (London, 1975), 643–76.

7. K. Elm, 'Verfall und Erneuerung des Ordenswesens im Spätmittelalter',

Veröffentlichungen des Max-Planck-Institut für Geschichte, 68 (Göttingen 1980), 188–238, on p. 195.

8. H. Grundmann, *Religiöse Bewegungen im Mittelalter* (2nd edn., Hildesheim, 1961), 524–38.

9. A. Vauchez, *La sainteté en occident aux derniers siècles du moyen âge, d'après les procès de canonisation et les documents hagiographiques*. Biblothèque des Écoles françaises d'Athènes et de Rome, vol. 241 (Rome, 1981), 427–8.

10. B. Ward (tr. and ed.), *The Prayers and Meditations of Saint Anselm* (Harmondsworth, 1973), 91. Date: R. W. Southern, *Saint Anselm. A Portrait in a Landscape* (Cambridge, 1990), 111–2.

11. Tr. B. I. Knott (London, 1963), 166. The first sentence in my version compresses a longer passage.

NOTES TO CHAPTER 6

1. E. Duffy, *The Stripping of the Altars* (New Haven and London: Yale U.P., 1992).

2. On confessionalization, see H. Schilling, *Religion, Political Culture and the Emergence of Early Modern Society* (Leiden: Brill, 1992); for the texts themselves, see M. A. Noll (ed.), *Confessions and Catechisms of the Reformation* (Leicester: Apollos, 1991).

3. *Opus Epistolarum Des. Erasmi Roterodami*, ed. Percy S. Allen, H. M. Allen and Heathcote W. Garrod (12 vols., Oxford 1906–58), 3, p. 376, l. 560: 'quid aliud est civitas quam magnum monasterium?' I am grateful to Professor James Estes for drawing my attention to this phrase.

NOTES TO CHAPTER 7

1. Don Cupitt, *The Sea of Faith, Christianity in Change* (London: BBC, 1984), 7, 9, 10.

2. 'Letter of Dr Wellwood' in *An Exact Relation of the Wonderful Cure of Mary Maillard* (London, 1730), 44–5.

3. For an extended discussion of Maillard's story, see my *Miracles in Enlightenment England* (forthcoming with Yale University Press).

4. Russell Stannard, *The God Experiment* (London: Faber, 1999), especially chapter 1.

5. Jon Butler, *Awash in a Sea of Faith. Christianizing the American People* (Cambridge, MA: Harvard University Press, 1990), 179.

6. Jon Butler relates these stories in *Awash in a Sea of Faith*, 184–5.

7. Quotations from Thomas Jefferson and Benjamin Franklin from *The Portable Enlightenment Reader*, ed. Isaac Kramnick (Harmondsworth: Penguin, 1995), 160–1, 163, 167.

8. David Hume, Note 10 in 'Of National Characters' in *Essays Moral, Political and Literary* (1742) (Indianapolis, Liberty: 1987), 208.

9. Quoted in *Race and the Enlightenment, A Reader*, ed. Emmanuel Chukwudi Eze (Oxford: Blackwell, 1997), 55–6, 57.

10. Butler, *Awash in a Sea of Faith*, 129–30.

11. Quoted by Butler in his *Awash in a Sea of Faith* 139, upon whose interpretation and illustration of these matters I have drawn considerably.

12. This description is to be found in the entry on Secker in *The Oxford Dictionary of the Christian Church* (2nd edn.) ed. F. L. Cross and E. A. Livingstone (Oxford: Oxford University Press, 1989).

13. Butler, *Awash in a Sea of Faith*, 133, 140–41.

14. Lawrence W. Levine, 'Slave Songs and Slave Consciousness: An Exploration in Neglected Sources' in *African-American Religion. Interpretative Essays in Religion and Culture* (London and New York: Routledge, 1997), 76.

15. John Toland, *Letters to Serena* (London, 1704), 15.

16. Frank Manuel, *The Eighteenth Century Confronts the Gods* (New York: Athenum, 1967), 66.

17. Edward Said, *Orientalism: Western Conceptions of the Orient* (Harmondsworth: Penguin, 1995 (1978)), 58–9.

18. *The Letters and Works of Lady Mary Wortley Montagu*, ed. Lord Wharncliffe (London: 1887), 289. I have drawn here on the ideas in my article, 'Gender and the "Nature" of Religion: Lady Mary Wortley Montagu's Embassy Letters and Their Place in Enlightenment Philosophy of Religion' in *Bulletin of the John Rylands University Library of Manchester*, Volume 80, Number 3 (Autumn, 1998), 129–45.

NOTES TO CHAPTER 8

1. Philipp Otto Runge, *Hinterlassene Schriften* (Hamburg, 1840–49), 1: 7, cited in Peter-Klaus Schuster, 'In Search of Paradise Lost', Keith Hartley *et al.* (ed.), *The Romantic Spirit in German Art 1790–1990* (London, 1994), 63.

2. *National-Zeitung*, 17 Jan. 1878, cited in David Blackbourn, *Marpingen. Apparitions of the Virgin Mary in Bismarckian Germany* (Oxford, 1993), 286.

3. William H. Young, 'An American Clerical Lanternist', *Optical Magic Lantern Journal and Photographic Enlarger*, vol. vi (1895), 135.

4. Philip Astor, 'A Surpliced Army. A Novel Way of Filling a Church', *Harmsworth Magazine*, vol. v (1900), 63.

5. *The Letters and Diaries of John Henry Newman*, ed. C. S. Dessain *et al.* (London, 1964–), vol. xix, p. 335: letter of Newman to Charles Meynell, 9 May 1860.

NOTES TO CHAPTER 9

1. David A. Shank, *A Prophet of Modern Times: The Thought of William Wadé Harris*, Ph.D. thesis, Aberdeen University, 1980, Part Three: Appendices, 868–9.

2. James R. Krabill, *The Hymnody of the Harrist Church among the Dida of South-Central Ivory Coast (1913–1949)* (Frankfurt, Peter Lang, 1995).

3. J. Jordan, *Bishop Shanahan of Southern Nigeria* (Dublin, Clonmore and Reynolds, 1949), 109.

4. Roland Allen, *The Spontaneous Expansion of the Church* (1927, reprinted London, World Dominion Press, 1949).

5. Thomas A. Breslin, *China, American Catholicism and the Missionary* (University Park, Pennsylvania, and London, Pennsylvania State University Press, 1980), 100.

6. David Paton, *Christian Missions and the Judgement of God* (1953, 2nd edn., Grand Rapids, William B. Eerdmans, 1996), 82–3.

7. Bob Whyte, *Unfinished Encounter: China and Christianity* (London, Collins, 1988), 296.

8. G. Stephenson, *Edward Stuart Talbot* (London, 1936), 114.

9. Dietrich Bonhoeffer, *Letters and Papers from Prison*, 5 May 1944 (London, Collins, 1953), 94.

NOTES TO CHAPTER 10

1. Rowan Williams, *On Christian Theology* (Blackwell, 2000), 38.

FURTHER READING

GENERAL

Sarah Jane Boss, *Empress and Handmaid: On Nature and Gender in the Cult of the Virgin Mary* (2000).

David L. Edwards, *Christianity: The First Two Thousand Years* (1997).

Adrian Hastings (ed.), *A World History of Christianity* (1999).

John McManners (ed.), *The Oxford Illustrated History of Christianity* (Oxford, 1990).

Norman Tanner (ed.), *Decrees of the Ecumenical Councils* (2 vols., 1990).

THE EARLY CHURCH

Peter Brown, *The Body and Society: Men, Women and Sexual Renunciation in Early Christianity* (1988).

Henry Chadwick, *Early Christian Thought and the Classical Tradition* (Oxford, 1966 and later edns.).

—— *History and Thought of the Early Church* (1982).

—— *The Early Church* (Pelican, 2nd edn. 1993).

W. H. C. Frend, *The Rise of Christianity* (1984).

Stuart G. Hall, *Doctrine and Practice in the Early Church* (1991).

Martin Hengel, *The Four Gospels and the One Gospel of Jesus Christ* (Harrisburg, Pa., 2000).

J. A. Jungmann, *The Early Liturgy to the Time of Gregory the Great* (1960).

R. A. Markus, *The End of Ancient Christianity* (Cambridge, 1990).

K. Rudolph, *Gnosis* (Edinburgh, 1983).

E. P. Sanders, *Paul* (Oxford, 1991).

LATE ANTIQUITY

Peter Brown, *Augustine of Hippo: a Biography* (1967).

—— *The World of Late Antiquity* (1971 and later edns.).

——*Authority and the Sacred: Aspects of the Christianization of the Roman World* (Cambridge, 1995).

Averil Cameron, *Christianity and the Rhetoric of Empire* (Berkeley, Ca. and London, 1991).

—— *The Later Roman Empire* (Cambridge, Mass., 1993).

Averil Cameron and S. G. Hall, *Eusebius, Life of Constantine* (Oxford, 1999).

Henry Chadwick, *Augustine* (Oxford, 1986).

Owen Chadwick, *John Cassian* (2nd edn., Cambridge, 1968).

P. Chuvin, *A Chronicle of the Last Pagans* (Cambridge, Mass., 1990).

E. R. Dodds, *Pagan and Christian in an Age of Anxiety: Some Aspects of Religious Experience from Marcus Aurelius to Constantine* (Cambridge, 1965).

E. D. Hunt, *Holy Land Pilgrimage in the Later Roman Empire* (Oxford, 1982).

Neil B. McLynn, *Ambrose of Milan: Church and Court in a Christian Capital* (Berkeley, Ca., 1994).

Anthony Meredith, *The Cappadocians* (1995).

Norman Russell and Benedicta Ward, *The Lives of the Desert Fathers* (1980).

Robert Wilken, *John Chrysostom and the Jews: Rhetoric and Reality in the Late Fourth Century* (Berkeley, Ca. and London, 1983).

Further Reading

THE EARLY MIDDLE AGES

Peter Brown, *The Rise of Western Christendom: Triumph and Diversity 200–1000* (Oxford, 1996).

Donald Bullough, *The Age of Charlemagne* (1965).

V. I. J. Flint, *The Rise of Magic in Early Medieval Europe* (Oxford, 1991).

K. J. Leyser, *Rule and Conflict in an Early Medieval Society: Ottonian Saxony* (1979).

Rosamond McKitterick (ed.), *The New Cambridge Medieval History* Vol. 2 *c.700–c.900* (Cambridge, 1995).

R. A. Markus, *Gregory the Great and his World* (Cambridge, 1997).

Henry Mayr-Harting, *The Coming of Christianity to Anglo-Saxon England* (3rd edn. 1991).

—— *Ottonian Book Illumination: An Historical Study* (2 vols., 2nd edn. 1999).

Dennis Nineham, *Christianity Mediaeval and Modern* (1993).

Henri Pirenne, *Mohammed and Charlemagne* (1939 and later edns.).

Timothy Reuter (ed.), *The New Cambridge Medieval History*, Vol. 3, *c.900–c.1024* (Cambridge, 1999).

J. M. Wallace-Hadrill, *The Frankish Church* (Oxford, 1983).

Patrick Wormald, *The Making of English Law: King Alfred to the Twelfth Century*, Vol. 1, *Legislation and its Limits* (Oxford, 1999).

EASTERN CHRISTIANITY

John Fennell, *A History of the Russian Church to 1448* (1995).

J. M. Hussey, *The Orthodox Church in the Byzantine Empire* (Oxford, 1986).

V. Lossky, *The Mystical Theology of the Eastern Church* (Cambridge, 1957).

Cyril Mango, *Byzantium: The Empire of New Rome* (1980).

J. Meyendorff, *Byzantine Theology* (1974).

Further Reading

Dimitri Obolensky, *The Byzantine Commonwealth: Eastern Europe 500–1453* (1971).

S. Runciman, *The Great Church in Captivity: A Study of the Patriarchate in Constantinople from the Eve of the Turkish Conquest to the Greek War of Independence* (Cambridge, 1968).

—— *Eustratios Argenti: A Study of the Greek Church under Turkish Rule* (Oxford, 1964).

K. T. Ware, *The Orthodox Church* (1963).

N. Zernov, *The Russians and their Church* (1978).

—— *Eastern Christendom* (1961).

THE LATER MIDDLE AGES

R. Bartlett, *The Making of Europe: Conquest, Colonization and Cultural Change, 950–1350* (1993).

Christopher Brooke and Wim Swann, *The Monastic World 1000–1300* (1974).

Rosalind and Christopher Brooke, *Popular Religion in the Middle Ages* (1984).

Caroline Walker Bynum, *Jesus as Mother: Studies in the Spirituality of the High Middle Ages* (California, 1982).

H. E. J. Cowdrey, *Pope Gregory VII 1073–1085* (Oxford, 1998).

C. Erdmann, *The Origin of the Idea of Crusade* (Princeton, 1977).

Richard Fletcher, *The Conversion of Europe: From Paganism to Christianity 371–1386* (1997).

George Holmes, *The First Age of the Western City 1300–1500: An inaugural lecture delivered before the University of Oxford on 8 November 1989* (Oxford, 1990).

J. Huizinga, *The Waning of the Middle Ages* (many edns.).

B. Z. Kedar, *Crusade and Mission: European Approaches towards the Muslims* (Princeton, 1984).

David Knowles, *The Monastic Orders in England, 943–1216* (Cambridge,

1940); and *The Religious Orders in England*, 3 vols. (Cambridge, 1948, 1955, 1959).

Malcolm Lambert, *Medieval Heresy* (London, 1977).

R. I. Moore, *The Origins of European Dissent* (1977).

Colin Morris, *The Papal Monarchy: The Western Church from 1050 to 1250* (Oxford, 1989).

Alexander Murray, *Reason and Society in the Middle Ages* (Oxford, 1980).

—— *Suicide in the Middle Ages*, Vol. 1, *The Violent against Themselves* (Oxford 1998); Vol. 2, *The Curse of Self-Murder* (2000); Vol. 3, *The Mapping of Desolation* (2000).

Jonathan Riley-Smith, *The Crusades: A Short History* (1987).

Beryl Smalley, *The Study of the Bible in the Middle Ages* (2nd edn. Oxford, 1952).

R. W. Southern, *The Making of the Middle Ages* (1953 and later edns.).

—— *Western Society and the Church in the Middle Ages* (Pelican History of the Church, 1970 and later edns.).

—— *Scholastic Humanism and the Unification of Europe*, Vol. 1, *Foundations* (Oxford, 1995).

Jonathan Sumption, *Pilgrimage: An Image of Medieval Religion* (1975).

The Reformation

Robert Bireley, *The Refashioning of Catholicism 1450–1700* (Basingstoke, 1999).

John Bossy, *Christianity in the West 1400–1700* (Oxford, 1985).

Euan Cameron, *The European Reformation* (Oxford, 1991).

A. G. Dickens, *The Counter Reformation* (2nd edn. 1989).

Eamon Duffy, *The Stripping of the Altars* (1992).

John Edwards, *The Jews in Christian Europe 1400–1700* (1988).

Diarmaid MacCulloch, *Thomas Cranmer: A Life* (London and New Haven, 1996).

—— *Tudor Church Militant: Edward VI and the Protestant Reformation* (1999).

—— *The Later Reformation in England 1547–1603* (2nd edn. Basingstoke, 2000).

Andrew Pettegree (ed.), *The Reformation World* (2000).

Menna Prestwich (ed.), *International Calvinism 1541–1715* (Oxford and New York, 1985).

Geoffrey Scammell, *The First Imperial Age: European Overseas Expansion c.1400–1715* (1992).

Keith Thomas, *Religion and the Decline of Magic* (1971).

A. D. Wright, *The Counter-Reformation: Catholic Europe and the Non-Christian World* (New York 1982).

LATE SEVENTEENTH AND EIGHTEENTH CENTURIES

Jon Butler, *Awash in a Sea of Faith: Christianizing the American People* (Cambridge, Mass., 1990).

W. M. Jacob, *Lay People and Religion in the Early Eighteenth Century* (Cambridge, 1996).

Phyllis Mack, *Visionary Women: Ecstatic Prophecy in Seventeenth-Century England* (Berkeley and Oxford, 1992).

John McManners, *The French Revolution and the Church* (Westport, Conn., 1969).

—— *Death and the Enlightenment* (Oxford, 1981).

—— *Church and Society in Eighteenth-Century France* (2 vols. Oxford, 1998).

Frank E. Manuel, *The Eighteenth Century Confronts the Gods* (New York, 1967).

Henry D. Rack, *Reasonable Enthusiast: John Wesley and the Rise of Methodism* (1989).

Steven Shapin, *The Scientific Revolution* (Chicago, 1996).

Further Reading

Deborah Valenze, *Prophetic Sons and Daughters: Female Preaching and Popular Religion in Industrial England* (Princeton, 1985).

THE NINETEENTH CENTURY

John Brooke, *Science and Religion: Some Historical Perspectives* (Cambridge, 1991).

Richard Carwardine, *Evangelicals and Politics in Antebellum America* (Yale, 1993).

Owen Chadwick, *The Victorian Church* (2 vols., 1966–70).

—— *The Popes and European Revolution* (Oxford, 1981).

—— *The Secularization of the European Mind in the Nineteenth Century* (Cambridge, 1975: 1990).

Ruth Harris, *Lourdes: Body and Spirit in the Secular Age* (London, 1999).

Adrian Hastings, *The Church in Africa, 1450–1950* (Oxford, 1994).

Hugh McLeod, *Religion and the People of Western Europe, 1789–1970* (Oxford, 1981, 2nd edn. 1997).

—— *Piety and Poverty: Working-Class Religion in Berlin, London and New York 1870–1914* (New York, 1996).

—— *Secularization in Western Europe, 1848–1914* (Macmillan, 2000).

R. Laurence Moore, *Selling God: American Religion in the Marketplace of Culture* (Oxford, 1994).

Albert Raboteau, *Slave Religion: The 'Invisible Institution' in the Antebellum South* (New York, 1978).

THE TWENTIETH CENTURY

Trevor Beeson, *Discretion and Valour: Religious Conditions in Russia and Eastern Europe* (rev. edn. 1982).

John Breen and Mark Williams (eds.), *Japan and Christianity: Impacts and Responses* (Basingstoke, 1996).

Further Reading

Tom Buchanan and Martin Conway (eds.), *Political Catholicism in Europe 1918–1965* (Oxford, 1996).

Raymond Firth, *Rank and Religion in Tikopia* (1970).

Adrian Hastings, *African Christianity* (1976).

——*A History of African Christianity, 1950–1975* (Cambridge, 1979).

——*A History of English Christianity, 1920–1990* (1991).

——(ed.), *Modern Catholicism* (New York and London, 1991).

——*The Construction of Nationhood: Ethnicity, Religion and Nationalism* (Cambridge, 1997).

Martin E. Marty, *Modern American Religion: The Noise of Conflict 1919–41* (Chicago, 1991).

E. R. Norman, *Christianity in the Southern Hemisphere: The Churches in Latin America and South Africa* (Oxford, 1981).

Roger C. Thompson, *Religion in Australia: A History* (Melbourne, 1994).

Bob Whyte, *Unfinished Encounter: China and Christianity* (1988).

PROSPECT

Steve Bruce (ed.), *Religion and Modernization: Socialists and Historians Debate the Secularization Thesis* (Oxford, 1992).

Richard Harries, *Art and the Beauty of God* (1993, repr. 2000).

Keith Ward, *God, Faith and the New Millennium* (Oxford, 1998).

Geoffrey Wigoder, *Jewish Christian Relations since the Second World War* (Manchester, 1988).

INDEX

Index

Index

Index